CHEATING DEATH

The 10 Thriving Life Principles

Cris Mattoon

To my beautiful bride, Kimberly, and our amazing daughter, Elizabeth, without whom my conception of love would be incomplete.

"Live the rest of your life as the BEST of your life!"

CONTENTS

DISCLAIMER

I am an imperfect man with an imperfect recollection. To the best of my ability, in this book I have tried to recreate events, locales and conversations from my memories of them. In order to maintain their anonymity, in some instances I have changed the names of individuals and places, and I may have changed some identifying characteristics and details such as physical properties, occupations and places of residence. This book reflects my opinions and is not intended to serve as professional advice or counsel in any discipline, including but not limited to financial, legal, medical, professional, or social affairs of the reader or any other individual or entity.

This book is not intended as a substitute for the financial advice or legal advice of trained and licensed professionals. The reader should regularly consult with a financial or legal professional in matters relating to her/his financial and legal affairs, and particularly with respect to any course of action that presents risks for which the reader is not currently informed or engaged. Like any activity involving finances or legal constructs, such activities pose some inherent risks. I advise readers to take full responsibility for their financial and legal well-being and know their limits.

This book is not intended as a substitute for the medical advice of physicians. The reader should regularly consult a physician in matters relating to her/his health and particularly with respect to any symptoms that may require diagnosis or medical attention. The information in this book is meant to supplement, not replace, proper athletic training. Like any sport involving speed, equipment, balance and environmental factors, physical activity poses some inherent risk. I advise readers to take full responsibility for their safety and know their limits.

Before undertaking any activities described in this book, be sure that your equipment, training, knowledge and preparation have been well planned and well maintained, and do not take risks beyond your level of experience, aptitude, training, and comfort level.

Although I have made every effort to ensure that the information in this book was correct at press time, I do not assume and hereby disclaim any liability to any party for any loss, damage, or disruption caused by errors or omissions, whether such errors or omissions result from negligence, accident, or any other cause.

BEFORE WE BEGIN...

1. Name one accomplishment that you are very proud of in your life?

2. Name one habit that is detracting from the quality of your life currently?

3. Name one person whose company you enjoy no matter what activity you are engaged in?

LIFE IN THE MIDDLE AGES

"Everything is an open book. I don't speak on other people's hardship, but if it happened in my life or something that has been an experience on my particular journey, I'm going to talk about it...I'm universal. You can relate to the things I say or that I go through."

~ KEVIN HART[1]

The drunk drivers, the strip clubs, and the semi-automatic gunfire hadn't killed me in my youth.

I had cheated Death, and for all appearances I had been winning at life. Not too shabby for a kid coming out of New York City back in the days of its financial and moral bankruptcy.

But as I approached what could be termed `middle age'—in my case 50 years old—I became acutely aware that I wasn't getting any younger. I had begun to read the Facebook posts about high school classmates who had passed away far too young.

I knew that I wasn't anywhere close to being ready to die, so I came to a realization that I had to up my game, resulting in my recommitment to live out *The 10 Thriving Life Principles* even more fervently.

The first small baby step that I happened to take was to resume distance running after a twenty-five year hiatus. Hence, imagining that I was racing against time and death, I adopted the imagery that each small step that I took to live my best life more fully was helping me to outpace that inevitable end that eventually claims us all.

The awareness that my life could—and should—be so much more amazing at this stage wasn't isolated just to my own experience. With increasing frequency, women and men would come to me for guidance with the *"Is this all that my life was supposed to be?"* question. Women and men from diverse socioeconomic, racial, cultural, educational, career, and familial backgrounds, who had achieved success by the standards of modern society.

Their yearning, their hopefulness, their experiences all fueled their desire to retain and enhance those aspects of their lives that were working well, while setting aside the expectations, trappings, and roles of the status quo that weren't serving any true purpose.

Perhaps you've felt that way yourself approaching this phase of your own life. Some (or many) parts of your life may already be amazing, but other parts of your life just aren't yielding the results you had expected. In a later chapter, we will explore the promise and the paradox that led many of us to this dichotomy in the middle years of our life.

You are not alone. In fact, you are _exactly_ where you should be at this moment. That's why you've picked up *Cheating Death: The 10 Thriving Life Principles*. You've got a whole lot of living to do before you come to the inevitable end. And, statistically, there is likely more than enough time left for you to live the rest of your life as the *BEST* of your life!

The Middle Ages—Then And Now

The Grim Reaper is a familiar archetype as old as time itself. Five hundred years ago, before nutrition, sanitation, and workplace safety became societal norms, the average lifespan was 31.3 years[2]. For those people who lived beyond childhood, adulthood provided but a sliver of time in which to find a spouse, bear and raise children to provide labor on the family farm or in the family business, and earn a sustainable living, before Death was waiting menacingly on the doorstep.

In the intervening centuries, Death has remained an unpredictable yet inevitable final frontier. While bubonic plague, marauding hordes from the north, and falling into unguarded machinery no longer stake a claim to most of us, modern women and men continue to meet an end generally not of their own choosing.

Life spans in the first half of the twenty-first century now top 78.6 years in developed nations[3]. Yet I continue to witness lives ending far too young among otherwise reasonably healthy, educated, and financially secure people.

Oh, they're not actually *physically dead*. These men and women have *simply stopped living*. You might even know some people like that (just asking for a friend). To the outside world, they may appear to be middle- to upper-middle class, but as contrasted with *The 10 Thriving Life Principles*, I simply refer to them as the "Zombie Class". More on that in a later chapter.

But first, I'd like to share a little about my own journey to cheat Death and outrun the inevitable.

I came to realize that there are no guarantees of another day of life. I also came to realize that life events form patterns that are more than mere coincidences. I have caused a lot of my own missteps in life, and still don't have it all figured out yet. That's part of enjoying the journey that you and I are about to embark on. Even better, you soon will come to realize that if a clown like me could be saved by *The 10 Thriving Life Principles*, then you will most certainly crush it!

◆ ◆ ◆

Living Your Own Amazing Life

Now it's your turn to pause and take action. Invest a few minutes to reflect upon these questions and when you are ready, write your responses in your *Cheating Death: The 10 Thriving Life Principles Journal* or in a notebook.

1. What are one or two aspects of your life that are already amazing?

2. What are one or two aspects of your life that haven't turned out quite like you expected?

3. What has led you now to realize that you deserve to live your life more fully?

JUST DON'T DIE

T he not-so-secret secret to cheating Death and outrunning the inevitable is to remain alive. Let's face it—what good does it do you to have a brilliant and well-financed plan to retire if you're not going to live long enough to enjoy it!

Worse yet, what if you *did* live a long time, but were in such poor physical health, with strained family relationships, and dire financial insecurity that you couldn't even participate in the activities you crave with the people you love? As we will explore throughout our time together, living is all about loving.

What good does it do to work so hard only to end up in the Zombie Class?

I'm a risk-averse person by nature, yet I've had several near misses with the inevitable, as well as lesser health signals over the years. And while I don't have cat-like reflexes, I may have received some cat-like good fortune, or what I attribute to my Lord and Savior just not being ready to take me home yet. The proof is that I'm still here, visiting with you on our journey together.

But let me be very clear. I don't know why I am still alive after some of the boneheaded mistakes I've made in my life. And even more stunning to me is how I sometimes survived near-misses due to one decision to act—or to *refrain* from acting. If an idiot like me has lived this long and figured it out, then you certainly will do better than me!

Pay attention to that small still voice within you. The same inner voice that today is telling you it's time to enjoy your best life with those amazing people whom you love so much, may also be that same voice that is going to *save* your life when you most need it.

To illustrate how a series of seemingly disconnected events in my own life drove home the point of how fragile and fleeting one's life truly is, I want to share some of my less-than-glamorous personal history with you.

Drinking And Driving Don't Mix

I have caused some of my own health incidents through sheer stupidity. Physical scars on my body are permanent reminders of my swan dive into alcoholic consumption as a teenager, and resulted from falling off a second-story deck at a friend's house. Not only did I *not* break my neck (or any other bones!), but I landed on some randomly placed sandbags from which I awoke hours later.

Although I drank myself into oblivion on-and-off for fifteen of my earlier years, I survived the ironic divergence of drunkenness and Death (or serious bodily harm) on multiple occasions. Other than generally adhering to my mother's wise admonition to avoid driving under the influence, I don't really know how I survived the sheer destruction that I wrought upon my physical and emotional self. My pastor has often said that there are 'no coincidences', so I've had to conclude that, as so beautifully sung by Carrie Underwood in her 2005 hit, Jesus literally decided to 'take the wheel'[4].

One New Year's Eve, I literally approached an intersection in life that provided me a brief hair-raising glimpse into a future that I would never want to be a part of. Home from college on break, instead of boozing it up, I found myself soberly chaperoning a friend's younger brother at his church's youth dance. This was odd in and of itself, because I wasn't really a guy who frequented church, and certainly not church dances, during that period of my life.

On our way back from the dance, only miles from his home, I was proceeding through a familiar suburban intersection when the light turned green. Instinctively, my eye caught sight of a vehicle barreling toward us from the left. As if in slow motion while slamming on the brakes of my mother's Buick Regal, I made eye contact with the older well-dressed couple in the large Cadillac as they sped by, running their red light awash in libations. I knew that a split second of hesitation on my part could have spelled a very different and gruesome result for my friend's family.

Strip Clubs And Rollovers

One decision involving one beer.

In my early twenties, I was making a living consulting in North Texas. One Friday afternoon, I had agreed to meet a client at a Dallas strip club on the Interstate 35E service drive. While no one would have confused me with a choir boy back then, I wasn't thrilled with his choice of venue. Strips clubs never have been the sort of place I voluntarily go to. And because I still had a 3 ½ hour drive that evening to make it to my mother's Houston apartment, I politely refused his repeated requests to join him in a beer.

I admit that I can be a judgmental person. These many years later, I still marvel at how a married guy with kids like him would choose to spend his Friday afternoon drinking beer in a strip club. But more importantly, for a guy like *me* who frequently drank beer, I had a gut feeling that having one myself would have been one too many. As I would soon learn in a matter of minutes, refusing that one beer likely kept me out of jail—or worse, from killing another human being.

I'm not certain that my client and I really accomplished anything during that strip club 'meeting', but the next few minutes would turn my world upside down. Once back on the southbound freeway, I was cruising along comfortably in the 55 miles per hour late afternoon rush hour traffic.

Suddenly, a vehicle swerved in front of me! I jammed on the brakes of my Mitsubishi Precis. Like a slow-motion movie that I observed from elsewhere, I watched as my car slid to the left and began to roll across three lanes of Interstate 35E.

The hatchback slammed into the concrete barrier that separated the freeway from the roadway below. Then the compact car ricocheted back into the southbound lanes of traffic, coming to rest on the driver's side. Vehicles came to screeching halts all around me.

When the chaotic motion stopped, I quickly realized that I had not hit a single vehicle on that crowded freeway—nor had a single vehicle struck mine. I was pulled from the car through the shattered passenger side window, and shook as many of the safety glass pebbles from my clothing and hair as I could.

Dealing with the highway patrol, emergency medical technicians, and tow company remain a blur. Amidst my shock, I was taken by a nice family of passersby to their home in Waco for a shower and a bite to eat. To make the night even more weird, I was then picked up by another client who was en route to Houston and later dropped off at my mother's place.

I never saw that Precis again. I would subsequently learn from the insurance company that the cause of the roll-over was a brake system malfunction, which had caused the brakes to lock up and pull my vehicle sharply to one side.

That one beer that I had declined at the strip club could have been the factor that suppressed my reflexes to turn the steering wheel as the car began to slide. One beer could have been the presumptive evidence that I had caused the accident under the influence. One beer could have introduced me—or another innocent motorist—to the inevitable.

Driving Under Fire

Gunfire doesn't sound the same in real life as it does in the movies.

I did not earn the privilege to serve in our military, and with the exception of musket fire at Independence Day celebrations and Civil War re-enactments I've attended, I had never heard live gunfire before. And certainly not directed at *me* while driving.

I don't consider myself an exceptionally brave guy, and I've been fortunate to largely avoid physical violence in my lifetime. But driving home from work in Detroit that December night, I again learned that you don't really know how much you want to live until strangers are attempting to deprive you of that option.

I had leased the Ford only ten days earlier, the result of a driver having totaled my prior vehicle while my wife shopped on Black Friday. I routinely drove a variety of routes home from my workplace to the freeway a few miles away.

Having taught bank robbery survival training for a number of years, I was attuned to be situationally aware. But it didn't take any specialized training to recognize that the dark SUV slowly rolling forward and bumping me at the urban neighborhood traffic light was no mere accident.

When the light turned green, I proceeded forward in traffic, keeping an eye on the rearview mirror. Sensing that the SUV was accelerating faster than I was, intending to make a deliberate second contact with my vehicle, I made a decision to turn sharply left at the next intersection.

As I entered the residential neighborhood, I heard the rapid popping sound hitting the rear of my vehicle. I accelerated. The SUV accelerated. And the shots continued.

I slid down in my seat and pressed the accelerator. The SUV sped up in pursuit.

As I ran through stop signs and red lights, barely aware of the blurs that were cross-traffic vehicles, I had a single thought in my head. I had a baby at home that I hadn't had a chance to watch grow up.

I had clarity now. I sped up even more. My pursuers were committed. They weren't just going to thank me for my keys and my wallet, and wish me well as I walked peacefully to a nearby payphone. I had already concluded that it would have been better for me to end up mangled in a high-speed multi-vehicle accident at one of these intersections than to die by gunshot if I stopped my vehicle.

Much as I don't know how those Dallas freeway lanes had remained clear as I rolled across them so many years earlier, I don't know how I managed to thread the cross-traffic unscathed as I ran Detroit red lights at 80 miles per hour that horrific December night.

I would later joke darkly with the dealership employee, when the tow truck lowered the vehicle from the flatbed, that it had earned its 'Escape' name that evening. But as I nervously looked into my empty rearview mirror and limped on two flat tires to a nearby well-lit shopping center parking lot off Grand River, with that dark SUV no longer in pursuit, I thanked my God ceaselessly.

The first to arrive on the scene were family members I had called. The flatbed arrived next, and I had to negotiate their willingness to transport my vehicle, so convinced were the tow truck drivers that my vehicle's current state could only have been the result of my own failed participation in some sordid activity involving drugs or prostitution. I guess that in an area of town where even tow truck operators must ride in pairs, they've probably seen all manner of white-surburban-dudes-gone-wrong.

The Detroit police officers kindly took my statement, asking some of the same sort of questions that the flatbed operators had. But since my story was easily confirmed with the time I had left the office, it became evident that I wouldn't have had any time to engage in shenanigans prior to arriving where I did.

A detective politely followed up with me by phone a few days later, offering scant hope based on my lack of assailant details, and that was unsurprisingly the last I ever heard on that matter. I had everything on that vehicle repaired, except the sole bullet hole that remained in the rear bumper until I donated the Escape ten years and 160,000 miles later.

In the end, I got to go home that evening to my beautiful bride, and I got to see my baby daughter grow up into the wonderful young lady that she is today.

Three times behind the wheel in three different decades.

Three different circumstances in three different cities.

Three decisions, a little luck, and a whole lot of belief in our Creator allowed me to live to see another day.

If you're keeping score: Cris three. Grim Reaper zero.

It would take me more than another decade to up my game against the inevitable. I guess I'm just a bit stubborn and have to learn by experience. But all along the way I've been learning to practice the principles to cheat Death and to live my best life.

In the chapters that follow, I'm going to share what I've learned and walk beside you as you learn to apply these principles in your own life. The thread that runs through it all is love.

◆ ◆ ◆

Living Your Own Amazing Life

Now it's your turn to pause and take action. Invest a few minutes to reflect upon these questions and when you are ready, write your responses in your *Cheating Death: The 10 Thriving Life Principles Journal* or in a notebook.

1. Have you had your own personal brush with death? If so, what did you do to survive the incident?

2. What event (or series of events) in your own history do you now recognize as something more than a fortunate coincidence?

3. Can you identify any behavior that you currently engage in that causes you unnecessary risk? Are you ready to commit to ceasing that behavior?

YOUR BEST CENTURY TO BE ALIVE

Thank you for picking up *Cheating Death: The 10 Thriving Life Principles*. Now it's time for you to live the rest of your life as the BEST of your life!

It's evident to me that you've reached a place in your own life where you've largely played by the 'rules', probably made a few mistakes along the way, but you're doing all right.

It's just as likely that you've also begun to question whether this is all that your life was meant to be. And you're ready to take action to more fully live. To live your most *amazing* life.

I believe in you and I believe in your potential to live your life more fully. I'm going to be your personal guide walking beside you on your journey. While we may not *yet* have met in person, I am confident that we *will* meet one day in the future. Might be at your workplace, at your church, at your school, or even sitting around your kitchen table.

I am glad that you've invited me along on your journey. We're going to have a great time getting to know one another better. I don't have all the answers. And my experiences may not resonate with all of your experiences. But it is my sole intention to support you and guide you on your journey with universal life principles. At the core of each of these principles is love. Without love, life remains elusive and unmoored.

To illustrate these principles, I will refer at times to experiences in my own life or the lives of others. You'll quickly come to realize that if someone who's made the dumb mistakes *I've* made can achieve some measure of success, then you'll have me beat hands down!

I began life as one of those stubborn, hard-headed people who generally learned best through experience, often painful. Perhaps you can relate.

As I got older, I got better at anticipating the outcomes of my actions before undertaking them. Life got better. Much better. I realized that it was time to commit *my* journey to paper when I recognized how often people were seeking my guidance to improve their own lives.

I live an amazing life. But let me be *very* clear here. This is NOT a get-rich-quick book. There will be no promises of social media stardom, Lamborghinis, or private jets in my tale. Instead, I've dedicated my time to living life more fully on my own terms. And I want to help you live your best life, too.

Who knows? Maybe your story will end up involving stardom, fast cars, and more. But your vision of your own amazing life may just as likely mean more time comforting an aging parent, helping raise your grandchildren, or volunteering in your local community.

The Better Half

I'll cut to the chase. We're all going to die someday. But so long as we're alive here on this Earth (or wherever you may be reading this), we owe it to ourselves and our loved ones to consciously be living our lives as fully as possible. But in order to live that most full life, you've got to take cheating Death seriously. Make your life the best century ever!

I intend to live to at least one hundred years old, and I am living proof that the second half of our century can be even better than the first half. Even as I continue to discover more deeply the richness of each of the principles applied in my own life, I believe that *The 10 Thriving Life Principles* can lead each of us to fully live the next five decades joyfully without regret.

Because life should be designed by intention and not plagued by misfortune or driven to a retirement necessitated by an artificial age threshold, I stood at that fork in the road for an extended moment before setting off on my own way. I'm still on my journey, and it just keeps getting better every day!

Much as I have guided and assisted others, today and every day I am here for you as you set off to reclaim the amazing life that you and your loved ones deserve.

I am going to share everything that I can with you that may help lead you to your very own fork in the road, and prepare you to take that next delicious bite of your future when you are ready. I'm also counting on you sharing your own insights and victories with me, so that I can continue to strengthen the universality of *The 10 Thriving Life Principles* when I speak with others globally.

Make The Decision

Yes, for me, the time I chose was the right time and the under the right circumstances. And I hadn't traveled this journey alone either. My beautiful bride Kimberly and brilliant daughter Elizabeth were walking (or perhaps, more appropriately, *running*) this next mile with me. We were laughing excitedly and almost incredulously, for having cracked the code. It all came down to learning and living *The 10 Thriving Life Principles*.

Please don't misunderstand my relationship to my successful career or to my personal past. I have been very skilled
at my chosen career, devoted to maintaining compliance with
financial, legal, and ethical rules and principles. Well-respected
in my industry for my passionate and consistent commitment
to actively fostering diversity, equity and inclusion in emerging
leaders, I have had the privilege to lead amazing teams of cre-
dentialed professionals and collaborate with countless more a-
cross the decades. I remain true to those rules and principles as I
continue to wake up each morning excited to seize the day.

But the day came. That day. Decision day.

My family and I had arrived at the decision to set aside those
aspects of life that didn't make sense, and to live life to its fullest extent while we remained able to wholly savor it. Embracing this decision was as plain on its face as deciding to plant a
spring garden when the weather forecast predicted gentle rains
in coming days.

For all of its randomness, life operates in a rather predictable
manner. I simply became more attuned to pausing, looking for
the patterns, and aligning my thoughts, actions, and timing
with those patterns.

Your Journey

My story is neither a fairytale nor a mystery. As in the prior
chapter when I recounted my three vehicular interludes with
the Grim Reaper, I am going to candidly share my life path with
you, cognizant that we each travel our own path to achieve
an amazing life. Hear me clearly—**I have made and continue to
make mistakes**. Death continues to nip at my heels.

Your life is unlike anyone else's life. How you reach the gateway to reclaim *your* amazing life and living life more fully on

your own terms will be as unique as your DNA, while sharing similarities across the larger human family. Let's do this together!

When you come to know me better, you will realize how many screw-ups I've caused in my own life. You'll figure out that *you* can actually reclaim your best life *even earlier and more easily then* I did.

As I looked back over my relatively young life, I came to recognize the countless self-imposed limitations that I created along the way as the overly-conservative by-product of being wired as a 'rules guy'.

Not only will you avoid many of my foibles, but you will be able to steer other loved ones away from today's equivalents. In my case, my daughter is a heck of a lot wiser and further along her life path than I was at her age, because she has learned from my own stumbles and scars.

Before we begin, let me reinforce that I'm not trying to talk you out of your career, or work in general, or earning money. I have remained engaged in all three of those activities to a lesser or greater extent where they serve my ultimate objective of living my amazing life to its fullest extent.

That being said, you'll notice that I reserve the discussion of finances until the latter principles. That ordering is not by chance. *The 10 Thriving Life Principles* are orderly and interdependent at the same time. Some will come to you easier than others, and they build upon one another even as they strengthen one another.

This journey to cheating Death and living your best life is about *you* and *your happiness*. I don't set a standard that for all people the acquisition of money, titles, fame, or possessions will make everyone happy. One or more of those things will make some people happier, while the abdication or absence of one or more of those things will bring peace and joy to others.

I am merely shining a bright light on the not-so-secret truth that *only you* can direct how much of your life you choose to live fully with the amazing people you most love and engage in the pastimes you most cherish. If you love to laugh, play, eat, and make the world a better place in the process, then we're going to have a good time together as you turn each page.

Thank you for picking up this book and inviting me to come along on your journey to reclaim the life you deserve! There will be no need to rush through each chapter, for you will proceed at the pace that suits you best. Just keep moving forward. Even so, you'll find yourself pausing and circling back to earlier chapters and to your journal to review your progress and tie the principles together in new ways before continuing onward.

Just like your decision to live your life more fully, partaking of the activities that you enjoy with the people you love, don't allow hesitation, doubt, or fear take the wheel.

Hesitation allows Death to overtake your body.

Doubt allows Death to overtake your mind.

Fear allows Death to overtake your heart and soul.

You could come out to your driveway tomorrow to leave for an important appointment, only to learn that the air ran out of your slow-leak tire.

You could come out of this world tomorrow, only to learn that the time ran out on your inevitable life.

Why take the chance with careless actions, stupid decisions, or delayed living? Why forfeit the game to Death? Follow your gut instinct and start planning now to be able to make the leap at the right time.

Trust me. Look left. Look right. Turn the wheel. Hit the accelerator.

Death won't be able to keep up with your passion for Life. Love trumps Death.

Made all the difference to me and my loved ones. What about you and yours?

The Tipping Point

It might strike you first as a crazy, random idea. But despite all of your personal and professional accomplishments, you may actually come to find (as I did) that you can improve the quality of your own life by living more simply, yet more fully.

You have reached a tipping point in your life. Something has happened (or failed to happen) that was the final straw. You know in your heart and soul that you *deserve* more, to live the most amazing life that you can imagine.

You likely have found yourself pondering one or more of the questions below.

☐ Do you want to spend more time with the people you love?

☐ Do you want to travel to the places that you dream about?

☐ Do you want to enjoy health and vitality in your most attractive body?

☐ Do you want to give more time and contribute more money to the causes that you believe in?

☐ Do you want to embrace more diverse viewpoints and skillsets within the teams that you lead, and advocate for the continued success of those who have earned promotion based on their merits?

☐ Do you want to retire early and do more of what you really enjoy without needing to set an alarm clock?

☐ What else would you love to do more of, have more of, be more of?

If you answered YES to one or more of those questions, and thought of additional areas of your life that you deserve more abundance in, then you recognize that you were made to live your amazing life more fully.

In the next chapter, you'll recognize how you got to this tipping point as we dig into the promises and the paradoxes we were told growing up.

◆ ◆ ◆

Living Your Own Amazing Life

Now it's your turn to pause and take action. Invest a few minutes to reflect upon these questions and when you are ready, write your responses in your *Cheating Death: The 10 Thriving Life Principles Journal* or in a notebook.

1. What was the most significant personal hardship that you've overcome in your life?

2. What is the tipping point or last straw that has led you to recognize that you deserve more out of your own life?

3. Is there a person, a place, or an activity that you daydream about when you think about living your amazing life?

THE PROMISE AND
THE PARADOX

In the first chapter (*Life in the Middle Ages*), I introduced our modern version of those women and men who ceased to live far too young. Perhaps in the prior chapter (*Your Best Century to be Alive*), you even recognized yourself or someone you know among the Zombie Class.

Upon closer inspection, these casualties of the modern success story have not intentionally shut down. No, in fact you have often achieved many of the outward signs of the good life. But as the years became decades and your thirties became the mid-forties or early fifties, you felt that nagging sensation that all the stuff, the titles, the hectic busyness weren't all that they were cracked up to be.

When I meet with women and men who are experiencing this awakening, there is often an initial retreat into personal justification. They will commonly tell me that they "enjoyed being busy", that it was the price one had to pay to "climb the ladder" and acquire things to "live the good life." The urgency with which they pour out their defense of their lifestyle choices makes their words sound more like they are trying to convince themselves than that they are trying to convince me.

Death deliciously devours denial.

I politely take it all in. But when we begin our work to-gether, I ask probing questions about their spiritual, physical, emotional, and familial health. Without fail, the cracks in the socially-acceptable veneer begin to appear immediately. And through those cracks seep sorrow, anger, loneliness, and regret.

It's healthy and liberating to say the words out loud, to express the feelings so that they can re-evaluate their past and redefine their future. We've got to go to those deep places sometimes, and you and I will go there in future chapters when you're ready.

The Promise

As the chapter title suggests, there is both a promise that we are made and a paradox that we are told. I don't believe for a moment that the people who made the promise to us intended anything less than the best for us.

I also don't believe for a moment that the people who told us the paradox intended anything less than the best for us. As my own life testifies, our parents, teachers, coaches, and em-ployers are good, hard-working people who have made a huge difference in our lives.

I have particularly benefited in my life because of the firm guidance of several committed and passionate K-12 educators, coaches, and others. I believe that many of these professionals truly cared for me and my fellow students and players. And without the genuine guidance and patriotism of our vocational educators and military recruiters, our nation would not enjoy its dominance in global technology, manufacturing and democ-racy. For each of those leaders, we should all be grateful.

On the other hand, the very same people often both made us the promise and told us the paradox. A common version of this well-intentioned dichotomy is found in the parental evolution of the Tooth Fairy imagery as a child grows older.

The promise makes sense in the early years to build up hope for the future (and perhaps some money under the pillow in place of the lost tooth). But eventually the child grows up and comes to learn that there may not have been a Tooth Fairy. While this benign tale of the Tooth Fairy may not be terribly traumatic for most children in its unveiling, nor lead to lost years of productivity and happiness as an adult, not all of the promises that give way to the paradox are quite so harmless.

Get A Good Education

If you grew up like me, and had at least one family member or guardian who loved you and cared about you, then you heard some variation of the promise from an early age. By and large the promise went something like this: *If you study hard and do well in school, then you will be able to get a good job that will support a family, allow you to own a home, go on some nice vacations, and retire well.*

For many of us who came from the lower middle-class, that promise translated into the American dream, and often represented the potential to earn, acquire, and provide more financial stability and opportunity than what our own families had fully been able to realize. I know that I certainly wasn't going to let them down. And I bet you felt the same way. So we worked hard to do our best.

The variations of "doing well in school" included excelling in academics or mastering a skilled trade. You made friends along the way, played some sports and participated in extracurricular clubs and activities. Your family made sure that you kept up your grades, treated other people well, and kept your commitments to your teachers, coaches, and employers.

In high school, you obtained formal guidance and informal

suggestions provided to you by family members, neighbors, teachers, guidance counselors, and military recruiters. These adults helped you to identify or validate your innate intellectual and vocational strengths to choose classes that would lead you to an appropriate institution of higher learning or vocational training. They told you all the time what you were *good* at, and how *successful* you were going to be.

You were steered *toward* certain classes and extracurricular activities, and either directly or discretely they steered you *away* from others. You didn't mind, because those adults knew what you were good at, and they were helping you to move forward to become successful. You certainly weren't going to let them down. They put a cap and gown on you one spring day, and you graduated with a high school diploma. Hopefully you had a great time. I know that I did!

After high school, you continued on to "higher education" at a college, university, or trade school, entered a skilled trades apprenticeship program, or joined the military to serve our nation honorably. Trusted adults paved the way for you with letters of recommendation, emails, and phone calls to connections at those schools or programs to make sure that you received the best educational experience possible.

We Love Our Teachers

Now don't get me wrong. I benefited from the encouragement and experience of many great teachers, coaches, academic counselors, and school administrators. I continue to believe that a significant majority of the women and men who educate our children and grandchildren today are committed to inspiring our youth to grow into the leaders of tomorrow. I also believe that our teachers and paraprofessionals invest themselves tirelessly into our children, but are largely underpaid for their level of commitment and responsibility in guiding our children intellectually, emotionally, and socially.

But I have also heard from the innumerable mid-career adults who have come to me for guidance and redirection, when they came to realize later in life that they had leaned their career ladder against a *convenient* wall instead of their *deeply passionate* wall. Some artists were meant to have become lawyers, and some lawyers were meant to have become artists.

Mission Accomplished?

While obtaining the education and skills, or soon thereafter, you launched into your career. You may have been fortunate enough to attend school full-time, living on campus, and perhaps holding down part-time jobs and summer internships. You may also have been working your way through school, attending classes at night or on weekends, while raising a family. Either way, you kept your eye on the prize and worked hard to keep up your grades, earn your degree or certificate, and never let your family, your teachers, and your role models down.

You got the good job. Now twenty-five or thirty years have passed. Like me, you are probably very good at what you chose as a career and you've risen up the ranks of authority and financial success. For some of us, the path that followed the promise led you into exactly the career that you love to this day. And even if you don't love the work you do, at least it pays the bills.

You have done a great job supporting and loving your family. You own a home, or at least you will when you one day (hopefully) can pay off the mortgage. You and your family have gone on some nice vacations, and have the social media photos to prove it. And, although it's well over a decade or two away, you feel good when you check the balance in your 401(k) and are confident that you will retire well.

So, what's the problem? What led you to pick up this book? I think you're getting a sense that for you the promise wasn't all that it was cracked up to be.

Maybe you have done very well, but suffer from the nagging emptiness that no amount of money, prestige, and material possessions can fill. Or maybe you're still struggling, and when you look up the line at your supervisor, you lose hope as you realize that she or he is still struggling and may not have found fulfillment either.

Either way, the future ain't looking too bright on the path that you're barreling down. The promise really didn't turn out the way that you thought it would. And no parent, teacher, or recruiter that made that promise of the good life to you is coming to save you now.

The Paradox

Maybe your situation isn't that bad. Your promise may have aligned perfectly with your inner youthful passion. If that has been the case, then I applaud you for having already lived an amazing life!

But more often than not, I encounter women and men whose apparent "success" shrouds the dusty, dormant, or dead dreams that they set aside to pursue the promise laid upon them by those well-meaning adults decades earlier.

When you were a child growing into your teenaged years, how did you play? How did you create? What did you daydream about during every spare moment?

Did you become what you dreamed of becoming? Did you build a career around what you loved doing in your spare time? Why not?

☐ Perhaps at some point in your life you were told that, "It's *not* all about *you!*"

☐ Maybe you were told that, "You have to be *practical*, stop dreaming, and go get a *real* job!"

☐ Likely some things in your life didn't work out the way you had planned, hoped, or intended, and either your or someone else said, "It's no use! I *told* you it wouldn't work out for you."

☐ What else were you told?

Guess what? None of that negative stuff people said (or you thought to yourself) matters now. It's a new day. In the words of Jon Bon Jovi...

"It's my life
It's now or never
I ain't gonna live forever
I just want to live while I'm alive..." [5]

It's true. You ain't gonna live forever. Your amazing life is a gift. And regardless of what you've done with your life up until this time, you are about to take control of your life like you've *n-ever* done before.

I know what you're thinking, *"Cris, you don't know where I've come from, what I've been through!"*

Yeah, you're right...to some extent. You *are* a unique individual, a human being created like no other. And I know that you ain't dead, so you've still got time to turn this life around.

I may not have met you in person *yet*, but I've met personally with amazing people from all backgrounds, all walks of life, and walked that journey with them as they've reclaimed the life that they deserve.

Poverty. Divorce. Single Parent. Prison. Addiction. Disability. Drop-out. Bankruptcy. Homeless.

Add what you will to the list. Perhaps I haven't person-ally experienced it myself. But I am committed to celebrating you in your uniqueness, and helping you to achieve the amazing life to which you are entitled. And even better, you already have what it takes to reclaim that life.

By the very act of you opening *Cheating Death: The 10 Thriving Life Principles*, I know that you are tired of the negativity. Tired of the excuses. Tired of the emotional, spiritual, and financial pain that you've been enduring. Tired of the regret for having laid aside your own dreams to pursue the promise that other people made on your behalf those many years ago.

You know how the promise has turned out thus far.

Now it's time for you to live your most amazing life, that life you envisioned in the pleasurable activities and mesmerizing daydreams of days past, and aligned with your inner passions of today.

◆ ◆ ◆

Living Your Own Amazing Life

Now it's your turn to pause and take action. Invest a few minutes to reflect upon these questions and when you are ready, write your responses in your *Cheating Death: The 10 Thriving Life Principles Journal* or in a notebook.

1. What promises were you told in your youth that led you to make the career and financial decisions that got you where you are today?

2. What activities and daydreams gave you the most pleasure in your youth that could have become alternative career and life paths?

3. If you could spend your time doing anything you wanted from now on, what would you spend your time doing? Who would you be spending your time with?

PRESS PAUSE, THEN RESET

S econd chances. Mulligans. Do overs.

Perhaps you can relate to the power of hitting the pause button, surveying your circumstances and surroundings, and then striking off in a new direction.

My own success has been the byproduct of fortuitous second chances. Sometimes I sought a change of circumstances to correct the course that my life had taken around me. Other times, I required change quickly because of some jackpot that I'd gotten myself into. Either way, I have always been a big believer in the power of starting over.

There are differing opinions among my contemporaries about whether or not you get do overs in life. Everyone's experience is different, and philosophies may vary, but I am 100% in the camp of second chances. Take all the second chances you can muster, because once the inevitable catches up with you, it's "game over".

This book isn't an instruction manual for getting rich quickly. It isn't a book about cheating the system or putting on a front to get back at those people who've doubted you and hurt you in your life.

But this book *is* about getting real with yourself and with others. This is a book about leveraging the power of love to cheat Death, and fully living your amazing life.

This book is a resource for the journey that you've wanted to take to reclaim the amazing life you deserve. I've been on the journey myself and I've walked this journey alongside others just as deserving as you. You're about to embark on your own well-deserved journey with me, so that you can make decisions and take actions to ensure that the second half of your century on Earth is your *best* half century.

You'll have to face up to your fears. You'll have to shut out the negativity that others cast your way. Others may enviously accuse you of thinking that you're "better than" they are, in an attempt to keep you exactly where you are. No need to listen to the haters or their rants. Remember, anyone can choose to come along and enjoy a most amazing life—if they're ready.

You'll have to let go of your own self-doubt and past failures. Everyone has failed at many things during their lives, so don't beat yourself up about your past. Heck, I continue to fail at stuff, because I keep trying things at which I'm not experienced or skilled—yet. Never be afraid of failure, because most of the time it ain't fatal!

We're moving forward and will only reflect upon the past when it uplifts or motivates us to take action. Remember, you're going to have to commit to making the necessary changes and put in the personal work required to live the most amazing life you deserve.

But before you and I plunge into taking action, it's important that you have an opportunity to pause and reflect. As you reclaim your most amazing life, it's not necessary to discard or change everything. It *is* crucial that you first identify those people, places, and things in your life that may be working just fine. Parts of your life may already be amazing. Then you can press the reset button *only* on those aspects of your future that you wish to upgrade.

Your pause can be as leisurely and measured as you need it to be. Change is hard and shouldn't be rushed or done haphazardly. Sometimes out of necessity, I had to create change slowly in my life as I continued to chip away at those things that had to be maintained in my daily walk. In some ways, creating change is like refueling a military jet while it's mid-flight over the ocean. You may not have the luxury of being able to set aside everything to redesign and rebuild overnight.

On this pathway to successfully transition from the old life built on the tired promise/paradox, you know that you will be following a path that others just like you and me have traveled successfully. Now reach forward to reclaim your most amazing life.

In the chapters that follow, you're going to be introduced to *The 10 Thriving Life Principles* to *Cheating Death*. I will share insights into how I came to understand each principle, the mistakes that I made along the way, and how I've come to apply each principle in my own amazing life.

I'm literally on this journey with you, and I continue to enjoy the benefits as I explore each principle more thoroughly. And I'm certainly far from perfect. I still don't have it all figured out yet!

More importantly, I'm going to provide you an overview of each principle and suggestions as to how you can apply each principle to realign your own amazing life. I say that they are suggestions, because although everything that I will share has worked for me or for someone else, I readily acknowledge that you are unique and seeking to live out your own inner passions.

After all, it's *your* amazing life. No matter how old you currently are, you are *alive*. But each day that you let pass you by without moving toward reclaiming the life you truly deserve is just one more day closer to giving in to the inevitable.

One day not of your own choosing, you *will* die. Rich and poor. Black and white. Women and men. Healthy and unhealthy. Happy and unhappy. Young and old.

Why would you leave a single day, a single hour, a single moment on the table unspent?

Wouldn't it make more sense to choose to live your most amazing life possible *before* you die?

Wouldn't it make more sense to provide your loved ones with the *best* possible shot at living their own amazing lives?

If this makes sense to you, then you've already begun the journey to reclaim your amazing life. Let's go!

◆ ◆ ◆

Living Your Own Amazing Life

Now it's your turn to pause and take action. Invest a few minutes to reflect upon these questions and when you are ready, write your responses in your *Cheating Death: The 10 Thriving Life Principles Journal* or in a notebook.

1. Who and what is already amazing in your current life?

2. What negative things might other people say to you when they learn that you have committed to improving your own life?

3. Who or what might you have to let go as you reclaim your most amazing life?

AN OVERVIEW OF THE 10 THRIVING LIFE PRINCIPLES

Living the principled life

"I only came to recognize the principles inherent to living my life fully, as I reconciled the many years of activity that I had undertaken to violate those very principles."

My life began to take a dramatic turn for the better when I came to accept that the amazing life must be built upon a principled foundation. The continued violation of principles spells repeated failure and eventual ruin for those of us who don't accept this core truth.

Death doesn't come to us suddenly, but slowly turns up the heat on the lobster pot into which we have descended until we no longer have the fortitude to climb out. Just look around you at the lack of success associated with most New Year's resolutions, fad diets, and get rich quick schemes.

And while I believe strongly that we each *must* have principles, I do not subscribe to the notion that we must all practice our principles in a uniform manner to be successful. Years of experience have proven to me that successful women and men often share several common principles, many of those being rooted in nearly every cultural tradition since the beginning of civilization. Other principles have evolved as cultures, social structures, and our collective knowledge of the human condition have grown. The common thread to each of the principles is love.

Love yourself at all times.

Love other people, including your family, friends, classmates, employees, and strangers.

Love your community, including the vulnerable and marginalized whom we may not yet know.

Love someone or something bigger than yourself, including justice for all of creation.

Personally, my adherence to *The 10 Thriving Life Principles* developed as a result of my own shortcomings, mistakes, and failures. Despite my innate stubbornness, I am not a person who enjoys causing or experiencing pain. Something deep inside me always yearned to live my most amazing life, and to share that life with other amazing women and men.

Even in its raw form during my youth, I guess you could say that I had principles. As I moved forward in my life, tripped over myself, fell down, and got up again, these principles became more clear, finally culminating in *The 10 Thriving Life Principles* to which I adhere. Principles can be described using various phrases, but I chose to focus my attention on those images that you can readily apply in your own life.

☐ **Principle 1: Speak Your Truth.** Take inventory of—and responsibility for—your past. Don't make excuses, recognize how you have lived your life up until this point, and acknowledge that your actions or inactions have led you to where you are at any given point in time. Love yourself as you are at this intersection of the past and present.

☐ **Principle 2: Accept Spiritual Peace.** You were created to live an amazing life. No matter what you have done or failed to do in your life, you are loved and afforded the grace to be at peace with yourself, with others, and with the universe. Each day provides a new opportunity to live in that peace. Love yourself for all the potential that you have to realize as you move forward.

☐ **Principle 3: Optimize Physical Health.** Your body is vital to living out your amazing life. You receive one body, so you must take appropriate actions or refrain from taking harmful actions to be able to live a long and full life. Love your body that is the physical creation you were granted to do great things.

☐ **Principle 4: Feed Your Intellect.** Learning can take many forms and it certainly doesn't depend solely on a formal classroom education. Much as feeding and caring for your physical body will extend your enjoyment of this amazing life, so too will continuous improvement of your mind and skills lead to a fuller life. Love your mind for its infinite capacity to learn and create anew.

☐ **Principle 5: Embrace Emotional Bliss.** Our emotions can exercise a great influence over how we live, how we regard ourselves, and how we treat others. Recognizing your emotions and understanding how past events may trigger your display of those emotions, goes a long way toward enhancing your amazing life. More importantly, expressing your emotions in a healthful manner toward yourself and others will deliver both joy and peace to all involved. Love yourself despite your imperfections and be open to receiving genuine and imperfect love from others.

☐ **Principle 6: Cherish Your Family.** No matter how your family is constituted, the friends and family members with whom you surround yourself contribute mightily to how you will enjoy your amazing life on a daily basis. Never take any person for granted. Embracing a broad definition of family only heightens your enjoyment of life. Love your friends and family members for who they are.

☐ **Principle 7: Expand Your Community.** Beyond yourself and your family is the greater environment in which you live, work, and play. You have special talents and experience that can benefit your broader community, and on a daily basis you can improve the lives of each person whom you encounter with a sincere smile and a kind word. Likewise, each person whom you encounter can add to your joy, knowledge, and well-being. Love each individual with whom you interact each day.

☐ **Principle 8: Extend Opportunity Equitably.** You have benefited to one degree or another from the opportunities that others have provided to you academically, athletically, professionally, and so forth. You can improve the lives of countless people in your community and in your workplace when you consistently uplift and advocate for those individuals who have put forth the effort and exercise the skills to compete for roles for which we make decisions or can exercise influence. Love and advocate for people whom you may champion and mentor, such that they will earn achievement meritoriously without regard to systemic bias and historical inequity.

☐ **Principle 9: Achieve Financial Security.** Money isn't everything, but it sure makes many things more accessible and enjoyable as you live your amazing life. Planning and providing for long-term financial security for you and your loved ones helps to eliminate a major source of needless worry, while also laying a firm foundation upon which you can strengthen your family, your business, your community, and your legacy. Love yourself, your family, and your circle of influence, such that you honor your professional and financial commitments, so as to enjoy the quality of life to which you and they aspire.

☐ **Principle 10: Define Your Legacy.** You can't take it with you. Your emotional, physical, intellectual, and financial achievements serve you well to live your most amazing life. But once you pass from this Earth, you can extend your impact to those people whom you love in more than simply material ways. Take the time to plan how you will deliver the most lasting impact for your loved ones and your community. Love your family and your community into a future in which you are no longer physically present.

I've ordered these principles in the manner that I've seen work well for many women and men, but you may certainly view them and pursue them in any sequence that aligns with your own choosing.

The 10 Thriving Life Principles are not tasks or steps to be achieved like virtual badges, checked off the list, and never revisited. No, as you'll see in the chapters that follow, you and I may never master the principles, but we will always be deepening our understanding and embodiment of them in our own lives.

By our humble and living example, others will be drawn into embracing *The 10 Thriving Life Principles* in their own lives. While you may not receive tangible credit for that effect, you will enjoy an even more amazing life knowing that you have helped others to live their lives more completely.

In future chapters, let's explore each one of these sources of principles in much greater detail. You will recognize how these principles have emerged and interwoven themselves through other discussions we're having in this book. More importantly, I encourage you to focus your attention on your own journey from pain to principles that currently guide your own life.

◆ ◆ ◆

Living Your Own Amazing Life

Now it's your turn to pause and take action. Invest a few minutes to reflect upon these questions and when you are ready, write your responses in your *Cheating Death: The 10 Thriving Life Principles Journal* or in a notebook.

1. Looking at *The 10 Thriving Life Principles* listed above, which ones appear to represent principles that are already present in your life?

2. What impact have your principles had in your own life already?

3. Which principle in the list above speaks to your greatest personal need at this time?

PRINCIPLE 1: SPEAK YOUR TRUTH

"Oh yes, the past can hurt. But you can either run from it, or learn from it."

~ RAFIKI, FROM THE LION KING[6]

We All Start Somewhere

My life certainly isn't a sob story, but every amazing journey has a beginning, and mine just happened to begin when my father and my mother split. I was around three or four years old the morning that my father, clothes slung over his shoulder, closed the Brooklyn apartment door behind him.

It was going to be okay, and I'd be living with him in another state by the time I began the first grade. At this moment, though, I was confused. After initially living in Astoria, Queens at my maternal grandparents' home following birth, we had moved to a few different apartments in three New York City boroughs, before taking the ninth story apartment across from Pratt Institute in the building beside that in which my paternal grandparents had lived for two decades.

I recall the apartment well, including a happy Christmas with a live tree decked out in stringy tinsel. That year, I had received a Fisher Price house, airport, and airplane. I particularly recall that our landline telephone had been installed in the closet, because my father wasn't a real fan of phones.

My parents didn't argue loudly. They just kind of fell together following high school. My father dropped out of college during his freshman year in Puerto Rico. I was born. Then they fell apart. It didn't have anything to do with me, but I didn't know that at the time. Notably, neither of my parents have ever badmouthed the other, and I am blessed to enjoy a close and loving relationship with both of my parents to this day.

Before my sixth birthday, I joined my father in Rhode Island and started first grade. We moved to another town and I attended another school for second grade, and another town for fifth grade, and another town for my first high school.

Moving around and changing environments became a pattern that would continue well into adulthood for me. Always in motion. Always running around or running away. I left my own trail of emotional, social, and financial wreckage in my wake of which I was not proud.

With inertia like that, it would take me a while to reverse course, slow the spin, and begin to speak my own truth. But without speaking my truth, I would not have been able to truly embrace and embody the remaining principles in my life. And that's why I'm very comfortable sharing this little slice of my early life with you. It happened. And I moved on.

What Does It Mean To Speak Your Truth?

Principle 1 is an inflection point, the first action that you take as you *Press Pause, and Reset.*

Speaking Your Truth embodies the notion that before you can move forward boldly and refreshed, you must be able to identify, fully acknowledge, accept, and discard those parts of your past or current circumstances that have been preventing you from living your most amazing life.

This is about getting real about your past and current situation on your way to an amazing future that starts today. You can't expect to cheat Death if you can't even get honest with yourself. To safely get real with yourself, you must grant yourself grace and practice patient love for yourself.

More than just a touch-feely exercise in self-reflection, to *Speak Your Truth* is to take a full inventory of, and full responsibility for your life with as much brutal candor as you can muster. As a starting point, you are not only seeking to catalogue the failings of others that have caused you pain, loss, and disappointment. You are obligated to identify your own failings that have caused yourself and others pain, loss, and disappointment.

Principle 1 has to be undertaken with the total objective of emptying yourself of everything, and only retaining that which is true, uplifting, and accretive to your amazing life. Like purging a musty cluttered basement or overflowing walk-in closet, you must be able to touch, embrace, and—where necessary—relive those memories, habits, and people one by one. Then you must let much of it go.

Importantly, you must exercise the confidence and courage to refuse to return the false, downcast, and degrading memories, habits, and people to your sacred life. Not everything requires an apology. Some stuff just happens.

Like the person whose clothing no longer fits her or his body type or fashion style, you must place the rubbish of yesterday in the bin of no return. This is a time for making no excuses. Own your past, give voice to it, learn from it, and in many instances, just forget about it.

How I Came To Speak My Truth

Throughout *Cheating Death: The 10 Thriving Life Principles*, I am sharing my unvarnished life with you. The candor with which I can speak about my shortcomings, disappointments, and outright failures is as easy for me today as breathing. But it wasn't always that way.

The confusion that plagued me throughout my childhood instability corrupted my self-concept and my worldview of others well into adulthood. I grew up making excuses, deceiving others, engaging in risky behaviors, and blaming everyone and everything except myself each time something didn't turn out the way I had wanted it to.

At different intervals in my life, I had brushes with the truth associated with digging myself out of holes that I had often dug myself. Physical wreckage. Emotional wreckage. Financial wreckage. In the early days, when someone called me to account for myself, I often ran away, uncertain of how to respond or what actions to take next. Only as I grew to embrace each of the principles, especially *Principle 1*, did I gradually achieve increasing levels of self-awareness that led to inescapable acceptance of accountability.

I'd love to tell you that I woke up one day, cast aside all my baggage, and embraced enlightenment...but that image would simply be a continuation of violating *Principle 1*. No, the reality is that I'm comfortable speaking my truth today, even as I continue to identify, reveal, and embrace deeper layers of my truth. I'm still happily on this amazing journey.

Taking Action: Speak Your Truth To Win Your Amazing Life

As with each of *The 10 Thriving Life Principles*, there is no one right way to *Speak Your Truth*. The first step is simply to get started.

You can proceed as slowly or quickly as you wish, choosing merely to dip your toe in shallow end of the pool or jumping right into the deep end in cannonball fashion.

I often find that women and men (myself included) prefer some form of written record, though that is certainly no requirement nor impediment to speaking your truth. Others choose prayer, meditation, speaking informally to a trusted friend, or engaging in formal individual or group therapy settings. You've got to do what works best for you.

Writing can take on myriad formats, including structured or unstructured journaling (including the companion *Cheating Death: The 10 Thriving Life Principles Journal*). Notebooks and blank journals—lined or unlined—work very well, too.

Women and men have shared their love of letter writing with me, with speaking their truth taking the form of letters to God, to deceased or living loved ones, to famous individuals whom they admire, and to a current, former, or future version of themselves.

Another written format that has gained great favor among many is in the manner of a 'dialogue' between the writer speaking with God, loved ones, or famous individuals to explore the layers of her or his past and current life to arrive at her or his own truth. Think *The Dialogues of Plato*.[7]

Some people retain the writings as a record of the transformation of her or his amazing life. Others engage in personally

meaningful rituals to effect the destruction of past fictions, excuses, and blame. Cast into blazing fires. Torn into tiny scraps
and left to drift into canyons. Tossed overboard into swirling
ocean waves. And so forth.

Again, there is no one right way. There is only your way at your
speed. You've made the decision to live your most amazing life,
and you know that your tollgate is making peace with a burden-
some past so that you can enjoy the journey that lies ahead.

So, whether you're easing along or running headfirst. Thinking,
praying, meditating, speaking, or writing. You are already engaged in living *Principle 1* in your own amazing life. Take your
time. Now let's take action to make it even more real.

◆ ◆ ◆

Living Your Own Amazing Life

Now it's your turn to pause and take action. Invest a few
minutes to reflect upon these questions and when you are ready,
write your responses in your *Cheating Death: The 10 Thriving Life
Principles Journal* or in a notebook.

1. What is your earliest memory of emotional pain, disappointment, or personal loss that you experienced in your own
   life? How has that incident impacted your self-concept and
   worldview of others in your present life?

2. What is your strongest memory of you causing emotional
   pain, disappointment, or personal loss in another person's
   life? How has that incident impacted your self-concept and
   worldview of others in your present life?

3. Who or what event has led you to recognize that it's time to
   Speak Your Truth in your own life? What is the ultimate outcome that you seek for your future self as you progress on this
   journey of truth and peace?

PRINCIPLE 2: ACCEPT SPIRITUAL PEACE

"I am not God."

Rebellion And Resignation

I am not God.

Let those words hang in the air for a moment. Because for much of my childhood and into adulthood, I acted as if I *was* the God of my own existence. In retrospect, while I couldn't possibly have been God, our Creator exercised a good deal of patience with me and regarded me with a sense of humor as I floundered about in the world.

This is neither a book about religion nor is *Principle 2* designed to evangelize you to my faith. I am unabashed in my own personal belief in the one true and living God. But I do remain humble enough to believe that when I join my sisters and brothers of all different faiths in the afterlife, I may come to find out that the Creator's name or other characteristics may not necessarily have been that of which I had been accustomed. Those details are not pertinent to the centrality that spirituality has played in my life journey.

Every faith tradition has some version of a parable about the individual who stubbornly sets off to find his or her own way in life, only to face setbacks that eventually drive him or her home to seek forgiveness. Christianity and Buddhism, for instance, shared versions of this prodigal son narrative. I have long embraced this story as a thread in my own downfall and rebirth.

I have always been loved and that love has been rooted in faith traditions passed down to me by my ancestors since my birth. In accordance with my maternal grandparents' faith, I was baptized at St. Joseph's Roman Catholic Church in Astoria, Queens as an infant. Other than possibly an occasional visit to a weekday Mass with my grandmother, I did not set foot in a Catholic church again until high school.

My father who raised me was Protestant, but without a strong leaning toward one tenet or another. Initially, I attended an Episcopal church, followed by Congregational, and then Baptist until age 14 when I just stopped attending altogether. Since I was attending without parents amidst families attending together, the seemingly central purpose of organized religion to bring families together in communion with God in worship was quickly lost on me, as it seemed I was simply sacrificing sleep and play time for no long-term purpose.

As I completed high school and attended college, I infrequently attended worship services, but when I did it usually coincided with an invitation from friends or a dating partner. I thus sampled another dozen or so denominations along the way.

My later twenties then became a period of professed belief in spirituality and searching for true meaning fueled by books ranging from Deism to Wicca, as well as major world religions. I settled into a realm of 'do no harm' as my central tenet of faith as I coasted along through young adulthood.

What Does It Mean To Accept Spiritual Peace?

Acceptance does not imply abdication of personal responsibility, but instead moves past wasted time bemoaning what has come to pass, and focuses upon decision-making and action that will improve the situation. Hand-in-hand with *Principle 1: Speak Your Truth* discussed previously, we grow to increasingly exercise acceptance with faith that God, a higher power, or the universe has ordained many solutions while according us a broad array of self-determination and free will. We need only to persist in our efforts to identify and execute upon those solutions through a principled exercise of free will. We come to love someone or something bigger than ourselves.

When you accept spiritual peace in your life, you receive the wisdom to know that you don't have all the answers—emotional, financial, spiritual, or otherwise. You receive the grace to live your amazing life imperfectly, even as I continue to live my amazing life imperfectly.

Likewise, you exercise acceptance with other women and men who are imperfectly traveling this journey with us. To accept spiritual peace is to embrace with comfort the knowledge that we don't have it all figured out yet, nor should we be expected to. But knowledge is powerful, and armed with our power of spiritual peace, we can cheat Death.

Accepting the spiritual peace in your life doesn't mean that you have to knowingly expose yourself to others who actively disrespect or dishonor you and all that you hold dear. Exercising your acceptance may mean that you have to separate yourself from harmful people, habits, or situations.

You receive the grace to get up each time you fall, so that you may continue your journey. Your life becomes more amazing incrementally as your faith grows stronger. Implicit in your faith is that you don't—and won't—know all the reasons why people act (or don't act) and things happen (or don't happen).

Peace is your touchstone, that beacon that lights your way along the journey or draws you from afar when you've strayed off the path. That peace is always yours to accept, so long as you never lose your faith that you deserve to live your most amazing life.

There is always more peace to be enjoyed than there are stumbles and failures to bemoan. Even in my own life, I was able to find redemption and come to accept that spiritual peace was available for me.

How I Came To Accept Spiritual Peace

My beautiful bride Kimberly and I sprinkled infrequent attendance at a New England parish into our lives before I slipped away again into law school studies as a convenient alternative use of my time. But the seed of my baptism and hers was to take root and lay dormant again until a few months before our daughter Elizabeth was to be born.

At a wedding for long-forgotten co-workers at a job my wife held years ago, we found ourselves in the historical Southwest Detroit parish of The Most Holy Redeemer on an October Saturday afternoon. Individually, we each felt the unmistakable presence of the Holy Spirit move within our respective hearts, drawing us toward our Lord God like the loving Father who intones that it is time to come home. When we spoke about our individual stirrings afterward, we knew that we were intended to raise our child in the Church.

We identified the parish within the city to which we had moved into our new home only a few weeks prior, and began attending the very next Sunday. Coincidentally enough, Kimberly had been baptized in that very parish as an infant. Over the next eighteen months, we both completed our remaining sacraments, including con-validating our civil marriage and baptizing Elizabeth, as we were fully received into communion with the Holy Roman Catholic Church.

During that initial time period and in the years that would follow, I opened myself up to the richness that true faith and boundless spirituality had to offer me. I let go of my childhood grievances and shunned narratives of warring faiths and the imperfections of established religious institutions.

Instead, I simply continued to speak my truth, and allowed myself to admit my own catalogue of human imperfections, scarred past, and ongoing struggles with self-improvement. And through it all, I simply let it go and learned that the broadest path to redemption would be through acceptance.

People die. Friends drift away. Financial challenges arise. Health crises emerge.

In the words of the familiar Serenity Prayer[8] that has long been a favorite of my father's, I ask always that *"God, grant me the serenity to accept the things I cannot change, the courage to change the things I can, and the wisdom to know the difference."* My approach to acceptance has literally saved my life on more than one occasion, and allowed me to move past significant financial and interpersonal losses without regret.

Acceptance also shifted my focus beyond everyday concerns and preconceived notions of success that appeared to plague many individuals around me. Especially after surviving an attempt on my life at gunpoint, I lost my attachment to material possessions.

This is not to imply that I traded our financial success for a pauper's cloak. We continued to enjoy the fruits of our labor and to direct our resources to create memorable experiences for our family. But we did dispense with many societal markers of prosperity, choosing instead to direct more resources to aid the less fortunate members of our local and global human family. I came to fully accept that the many blessings that had been abundantly poured out on my family were not meant solely to sustain or enrich our household, but were our stewardship to administer for the good of others.

Having overcome personal obstacles to earn an advanced education and attain significant success in my career, I clearly saw that my redemption lay in giving it all away—emotionally, intellectually, and financially—to lift up my sisters and brothers. As our Pastor reminds us each week, we must "put our faith into action".

Taking Action: Accepting Spiritual Peace To Win Your Amazing Life

Whatever your conception of spirituality is—centered around a deity, natural forces, or atheism—I implore you to pause and consider what the redemption of spiritual peace here on Earth is for you and your loved ones.

You deserve to experience abundant love, to enjoy the abundant fruits of your labor, of your investments, to your heart's content. Every one of us has our own inner vision of what our personal paradise looks like, tastes like, feels like. As I have found through my own amazing life, you already possess that ability to attract the people and to marshal the resources to experience your version of paradise.

Accepting spiritual peace in your own life will likely result in actually multiplying your love and abundance when you let go of the pursuit of materiality, and instead focus your efforts on accepting yourself and others in their imperfection, such that you create the most opportunity for others to flourish on their journey with you.

On my own spiritual journey, I have not let up on my work ethic in any area of my life, but I did begin to consciously weave into each decision and activity an objective to engage and empower others. I used every interaction as an opportunity to further other women and men in their own lives. I used every interaction as an opportunity to demonstrate non-judgmental love as modeled for me by our Creator. And I continue to do it imperfectly, lapsing into old habits at times when I have failed to live up to those aspirations.

I have experienced many personal challenges, and beyond those that I experienced myself have I been consulted by others wrestling with their own challenges.

Health. Family. Education. Career. Discrimination. Finances. Sports. Life Strategies. Recovery. Second Chances.

Where I was led by the Spirit, I would go even if I didn't entirely understand why I was being called to provide assistance. Sometimes the only resources I could offer were love, compassion, and nonjudgmental understanding. Often I was led to someone who was enduring a challenge that I myself had endured in my own life, simply so that I could offer hope that there would be light at the end of the uphill climb out of the mineshaft.

I am not God. You are not God.

We are simply imperfect women and men on this amazing life journey who have been fortunate enough to be saved—physically, emotionally, spiritually—by the grace of God or nature.

My redemption is in pausing as often as possible to lend a helping hand to women and men who want to exercise their own self-discipline to improve the situation in which they find themselves. Coaching. Mentoring. Volunteerism. Financial contribution.

You will need to figure out what redemption means to *you*. I can assure you that you will more quickly attain and live more fully your amazing life when you have helped enough other people to regain spiritual peace in their lives.

Living Your Own Amazing Life

Now it's your turn to pause and take action. Invest a few minutes to reflect upon these questions and when you are ready, write your responses in your *Cheating Death: The 10 Thriving Life Principles Journal* or in a notebook.

1. What is your earliest memory of spiritual peace in your own life? What spiritual tradition did you practice in childhood?

2. What event(s) in your life led you away from spiritual peace? How did you feel as spiritual peace slipped away from you?

3. Who is someone in your life or in the public realm that exhibits a level of spiritual peace that is attractive to you or conducive to your personality? What is one action you could take to connect with that individual?

PRINCIPLE 3: OPTIMIZE PHYSICAL HEALTH

I t's hard to fully live your amazing life and retire early if you're dead.

But it's made even harder if you're currently and consistently wasting your income on frequent co-pays, maintenance prescriptions, and lost work time. My physician rarely needs to see me and my pharmacy is simply a convenient place to get the occasional vaccine. But it wasn't always that way for me.

Russian Roulette

"The test results came back. You're pre-diabetic and your bad cholesterol is at unhealthy levels," my family physician began. "I'll prescribe a statin."

"Thanks, Doc, but I'm not really into drugs to reverse something I caused. What can I do to fix this?"

And so this leg of my journey began in my early forties.

The signs were there years earlier. I had returned from my honeymoon at my highest lifetime weight. My wife had married a fat guy who thought he was still that skinny high school cross country runner with a teenaged metabolism.

Throughout my thirties into my forties, I conned myself into believing that my diet of "healthy" crunchy snacks and starches (pasta, potatoes, bread) were fine. At least I wasn't eating fast food, vending machine snacks, and deep fried everything. I walked around the neighborhood and occasionally enjoyed a span at a local gym, before allowing life to again get too "busy".

I would eat like this, because our family life was busy and I justified that my brown bag lunch was "healthier" and "less expensive" simply because I wasn't eating out or going to the cafeteria every day. I would come to find out that I was wrong on both accounts, and you may have come to that conclusion too.

On that mid-winter day, the facts were as cold and hard as the frozen ground outside the doctor's office. We established that the supposedly "healthy" carbohydrates I so depended upon were exactly what my body converted into excess cholesterol, sugar, and fat. I had been slowly, happily killing myself from the inside out.

I committed to my doctor that I would make lifestyle changes and we agreed I'd return in 90 days for more bloodwork.

I've always loved a good challenge. I immediately researched healthy food choices that would replace my death diet, went shopping for new foods and stuck to the plan.

When the next round of bloodwork came back 90 days later, my doctor was incredulous.

*"I've never had a patient make this much progress without
the aid of a statin in such a short period of time. Not only
are you out of danger for diabetes, but you've improved your
cholesterol numbers to return to a healthy range."*

We talked about the approach that I had taken (fresh vegetables, lean meat and plant-based proteins, largely gluten-
free and natural carbs). Virtually eliminating processed foods
from my eating plan has likely had the largest impact on my
health. Allergies, digestive issues, lethargy, and more largely
self-corrected themselves.

What Does It Mean To Optimize Your Physical Health?

The point of living an amazing life is to *fully* live your life. It
makes little sense to make grand plans with the people you love
and acquire the financial means to execute your plans, but not
have the physical capacity to undertake your plans.

Optimizing your physical health involves achieving the stamina, strength, and constitution to support your bucket list of activities, while protecting yourself from and reducing the negative effects of internal and external physical health threats. You
can't cheat Death and live your most amazing life, if you continue to practice a lifestyle that is an open invitation to Death
to camp out at your bedside. You will come to love the physical
body with which you have been blessed.

Each individual can decide what is the optimal level of health
that she or he seeks, but at a minimum one should be able to
enjoy chosen activities without suffering from a lack of physical preparedness or a compromised immunity to environmental factors. This isn't about fat-shaming and all of the other
politically correct fads, but is about long-term sustainable satisfaction with your body and its health.

Countless individuals have amply demonstrated that physical and biological challenges may be overcome through committed and consistent actions. Others may make excuses about their own perceived limitations, but when the blind have summited Mount Everest, amputees have earned gold medals in international sports competitions, and sickly children have grown into international outdoorsmen and national leaders, I am confident that you would not have picked up this book if you didn't relate more to the winners than to the whiners.

How I Came To Optimize My Physical Health

The tenets that support my execution of *Principle 3* and have transformed my own physical presence are best summed up in the phrase "Protect, Extend, and Enjoy". This theme reflects my journey, and may differ slightly or greatly from your own physical principles.

Protect

I grew up as a short, slightly-built youth. Among classmates and in the neighborhood, I was often one of the smaller kids. But I enjoyed participating in sports and other activities, so I can vividly recall the experience of getting the wind knocked out of me during a backyard tackle football game where I found myself crushed beneath Skippy, my older neighbor whose own weight was likely double mine. That experience didn't stop me from playing football, but it did help me to focus on my footwork and speed to a greater degree, so as to mitigate the future frequency of ending up on the bottom of the proverbial pig pile.

Similarly, I played basketball at recess for several years. I compensated for my stature with my scrappiness to compete for rebounds, resulting in the occasional elbow or ball striking my face. In another instance, I landed hard on top of an opponent's foot, only to sprain my ankle as it rolled sideways on my way to the asphalt. Again, these experiences didn't stop me from playing basketball, and I was surprised to learn years later that my nose had actually been broken in two different places!

I learned to focus on *protecting* my physical body, not by removing myself from physical engagement, but by improving those competitive skills that would reduce (*not eliminate*) the risk that I would suffer physical injury or discomfort.

When I coached my daughter and others in soccer, football and basketball years later, I didn't teach her or her teammates to fear injury. Keeping safe play first and foremost, I simply focused my attention on imparting skills and tactics that served to optimize their talents. When the occasional injury did occur from playing assertively, the players' attitudes generally reflected a hunger to heal and return to active play and competition. Winning attitudes heal faster and return athletes to play sooner and better informed about how to minimize the risk of similar injuries in the future.

Extend

I am skilled at far fewer physical activities that those for which I am ill suited. While it's always fun to engage in group activities or be challenged by new activities, I have also come to recognize that I excel in some more than others.

When friends or family members invite me into a friendly softball or volleyball game, I know that the social opportunity for togetherness, laughter, and good-natured competition are among the key benefits. Given the infrequency with which I play either sport, my lack of practice, and the spontaneity of the occurrence may not result in me becoming inspired to take up the sports daily. I'll enjoy the game, give it my best effort, laugh a lot, and be glad that I participated.

As a youth, I did identify that I had an aptitude and enjoyment of running. And while my short bursts of speed were generally sufficient to power me through a baseball or basketball game, I didn't enjoy sprinting enough to take up soccer or short-distance track events. I have no idea how I placed or what time I logged, but I do recall the joy and comfort that I felt the first time I competed in a one-mile race in Explorer Scouts.

Distance running. No physical contact. Individual dependency. Competition against both self and others. Mind left free to focus on other ideas while the body did the work. Perfect fit for me.

I enjoyed the sport as a high school cross country runner and continued running 5Ks into young adulthood. Though I allowed running to slip away from me for nearly 30 years, when I picked it up again, it slipped on nearly as easily as well-fitted clothes or shoes.

For me, distance running is where I optimize my physical principles. Enhanced by weight training and conditioning, running provides me a core activity that strengthens me across multiple principled dimensions. I challenge myself to develop greater stamina and log more miles than before. By living in accordance with my physical principles, I am unleashed to extend my life more fully. I am literally outrunning the inevitable!

Enjoy

I live by the physical principle that if you got it, flaunt it. You may feel very differently and choose to be more reserved with your physique, and I can respect that.

My frame of reference stems from the belief that our Creator provided me with this wonderful body to use to its maximum potential for the relatively limited time that I am here on Earth. I have been entrusted with a stewardship to care for and maintain it, and to use it for the good of others. Often the most good that I am doing in terms of physical principles is to help others overcome the physical challenges that they are experiencing.

I am not a doctor nor a licensed physical trainer. Women and men come to know that I returned to my pre-college weight through self-discipline and simple science. My own family physician deems my physical age to be more than ten years younger than my chronological age.

You've got plenty to look forward to. I am living proof that if an average guy like me could let myself go, get fat, become pre-diabetic and dangerously cholesterol-ridden, only to reverse it all and run marathons, then you should know that you can do ANYTHING!

Closely related to my internal health and weight loss is my comfort with my physical appearance. Yeah, I know that my bony nose has bumps that chronicle the self-healed breaks. Sure, I'm under six feet tall. So what?!

I look amazing! I take care of my skin, my hair, my smile. I put on well-fitting clothes and dress how I want to dress. I don't hide in loose-fitting, ill-fitting clothes because of some feigned societal sense that we shouldn't be showing off who we are. Heck, through the grace of God, I earned this body. When I go out to dinner or to the beach, why would I want to hide myself?!

I've had women and men come up to me just to tell me that they started eating differently, gave up smoking, began an exercise program, because they figured if I could do it, they could, too. For themselves. For those people whom they love. And they are succeeding at it!

So can you. One step at a time. One bite at a time. One day at a time.

From a principled point of view, if you're not willing to take care of the one body that your Creator provided you, then perhaps you are relying too heavily on life insurance. Don't you want to be alive and vibrant enough to enjoy running around with your children or grandchildren?! Either way, you have to make sure that your family is well taken care of, if you won't choose to exercise the self-discipline to practice physical principles in your life.

Taking Action: Optimizing Your Physical Health To Win Your Amazing Life

Maybe you are in optimal physical condition, a regular Mr. Olympia or Miss America. If you are, I applaud you for your self-discipline and follow-through. If you're like most of the rest of us, read on.

You know that I'm not a dietician or a medical doctor, and each one of us has unique physical and dietary requirements, so I'm not going to pontificate on one food plan or exercise plan over another. Your very first step before taking any radical action with diet or exercise is to make an appointment and visit with your family physician.

If you think that you could be doing better with your eating habits, I encourage you to visit your family physician. Ask her or him to recommend a nutritionist. And do your homework. Try as many varieties and options for physical exercise and eating plans as you wish to determine what works best for you. *Any* positive step is better than doing nothing at all to improve. Frankly, I don't think you'd be reading this if you weren't tired of relying upon your old excuses for being out of shape.

"But, I Don't Like Vegetables!"

I'm a big believer in making incremental changes over time. While I chose to tackle my own immediate health scare in the first 90 days, my progress continued over the span of months and years. I swapped out foods one for another, gradually, finding items I liked or grew to like. Avoided others. I made choices.

In addition to food, I parted ways with sugary "fruit" juices and diet soft drinks. When you start reading labels, and realize how many man-made factory chemicals are in so-called healthy beverages and foods, you begin to imagine how much better off you might be without them.

And while I have no prudish moral opinion about consuming alcoholic beverages, I chose to part with my moderate love of beer, wine and cocktails several years ago. That is not to say that I may not one day decide that I'd like to enjoy a nice adult beverage on a warm sandy beach, but the urge just doesn't align with the lifestyle that I've created.

Make eating well a game. I came to call my choices of food and beverage the "90/10 plan". I eat well 90% of the time, so that the other 10% of the time it doesn't matter what I eat. Perfection is often the enemy of greatness. Besides, embracing imperfection removes excuses for quitting on a positive lifestyle simply because you fell off the wagon at a buffet or party. I never beat myself up about what I eat, because I ain't perfect. It's 90/10 all the way for me! Remember, I'm back to my pre-college weight and waist size.

Keep track of what foods and beverages you've eliminated and those that you've come to love. Celebrate these new flavors and new dishes with family and friends. Make them and share them at family events and church pot lucks.

Allow yourself cheat days and guilty pleasures. Accept offers of cake at birthday parties and fresh-baked cookies or pie at social events. There's no reason to insult someone's hard work or good will trying to eat perfectly. *The 10 Thriving Life Principles* are about a balanced approach to loving yourself while cheating Death, and part of that balance is found by participating as fully as you are able in the social events that you enjoy with your family and the broader community. Social events that often involve food.

I never use time as an excuse not to eat healthfully. But while I endeavor to plan my meals and prepare my foods for optimal daily health, I also recognize that business travel, conferences, vacations, and other events will occasionally impact the availability of your preferred choices. An occasional muffin, glass of sugary juice, or fried chicken hasn't killed me.

The point is, do the best you can and stop making excuses for physical ailments and conditions that you've caused through your own mindless eating habits. You can continue to eat fast food at your cubicle until age 65, or you can retire early and well-funded on a beach somewhere. But you aren't likely going to do both.

You can spend your money on co-pays, all manner of prescriptions and over-the-counter remedies, and lose wages or time for sick days. Or you can practice some self-discipline, trade consuming processed food for healthier alternatives, and save enough money to choose your own retirement lifestyle.

I don't know about you, but Aspen sounds better than acid reflux, and Miami sure beats Mylanta.

Get Moving!

Eating well was only going to take me so far.

While I had remained physically *active* as a do-it-your-selfer and youth athletic coach, I wasn't engaging in enough physically demanding activity on a consistent basis to fully optimize my health. I could move dump truck loads of gravel around my property to build a paver patio, and I could run the basketball court all winter, but in between projects and seasons, I wasn't doing anything to challenge Death.

I have always taken notice of the stories of men in their 40s, 50s, and 60s who die unexpectedly, leaving behind a family. Those stories are hitting a little closer to home now, as high school and college classmates have begun to succumb. During the recent global COVID-19 pandemic, it had been noted by scientists that high blood pressure and obesity—both largely preventable self-inflicted maladies of modern laziness—dramatically increased one's susceptibility to dying from the virus.

And while I have always maintained enough life insurance to financially protect my own family, there's really not a dollar figure that I could place on the future decades that we'd like to enjoy with one another on this side of the pearly gates.

Just Don't Die!

In the year that I was going to turn 50, I was out walking our dog in the neighborhood one cold winter night. For some reason, I decided to jog the next block, and then the next. At that moment, after a 25+ year hiatus from regular running, I committed to train for a 5K that is held in our city each summer.

I didn't do much jogging the remainder of the winter, but as spring began, I initiated a slow, progressive program of running. It wasn't miraculous, and in fact I probably looked awkward, but I gradually improved my endurance. I registered for that 5K, and walked the few blocks from our house to the starting line with one goal in mind: *Just don't die!*

I don't recall what my race time was that day, but not only didn't I die on the course, but I also didn't finish last. My beautiful bride and amazing daughter were both there near the finish line cheering me on. I had so much fun that I began entering other 5K races and worked my way up to 10Ks. In fact, the same friend who accompanied me on my first 10K also encouraged me to run my first half marathon with him.

I enjoy the physical, emotional, mental, and spiritual benefits of running. I can do it anywhere, and always take my shoes and gear on business trips and vacations, getting in as many miles as possible. I've found running to be a great way to explore new territory and meet many interesting people.

I have found that running outside in the winter has significantly expanded my lung capacity and reduced my susceptibility to viral infections, also noted as inhibitors to suffering the more severe effects of COVID-19. In addition to running, my family and I engage in cardiovascular and strength training activities at our local fitness center for added fun and physical health.

Running and strength training work well for me and have helped me to further strengthen and protect my own body from unnecessary ailments, thus reducing my financial outlay for physicians, prescriptions, and downtime.

Do Something!

"But, Cris, I don't like to run..."

Would you like some cheese to go with that whine?

I'm not telling you that you have to *run* to reclaim your health. I don't have an endorsement deal to promote any one brand of running shoes or the sport in general. I also enjoy golf, soccer, resistance training, and other physical activities.

I am telling you to do *something*. Like the Nike slogan says, "Just do it!" Go visit your doctor before engaging in any new exercise plan (remember, Cris is a doctor of juris prudence and NOT a medical doctor). Just don't sit there, younger than me, and allow me to run laps around your lazy butt! Any form of consistent physical exercise is going to reduce your risk of obesity and many other conditions. Obesity is a killer choice in the long run, so why put up with it?

I am suggesting that healthful eating and physical activity complement each other well, and are likely to increase your overall quality of life, while reducing your financial expenditures for family medical care. I include the family, because if you are purchasing and preparing healthier meals and engaging in physical activity as a family (even different individual activities), then you can't help but enjoy the benefits as a family.

On the contrary, we all know that family where the kids and the parents always seem to be sharing sickness all year long, one cold, flu, or sinus infection after another. Those sick days missed from work or school, those co-pays, laboratory tests, and prescriptions add up. It becomes a cycle of sickness that benefits absolutely no one. Not only do I not want to *be* that family, but I *avoid* families like that, because I don't want what they've got. And it's largely preventable.

Think about the exponential financial impact of saving and investing 75-90% of your current family medical expenses into fun vacations and your early retirement. And then continuing to maintain low medical expenses post-retirement that allow you to spend more of your money doing the things that you *enjoy*! Personally, I prefer Paris to the proctologist.

What's Next?

I encourage you to take some time to consider your current physical ailments or inconveniences.

Take a look inside your refrigerator, freezer, cupboards, and pantry.

Take a look at your waistline and your wardrobe.

Speak your truth about yourself to yourself.

Make some new decisions.

Make a new grocery list.

Make time to engage in a physical activity that makes you sweat.

True, we've had to purchase new clothes in our family to fit our slimmer waistlines and firmer bodies, but that investment in looking good and feeling great—physically, mentally, emotionally, and spiritually—is but a small price to pay to retire early and live the lifestyle of your own making. And you can even donate those larger clothes to a local charity and possibly qualify for an income tax deduction like we do (*of course, I am not advising you regarding tax matters, so you will have consult your own income tax advisor*).

This physical transformation is about you employing consistency over the course of time. Your physical health didn't decline in a day, a week, or a month. So, give yourself a break and accept that you will be restoring your amazing physical health one step at a time. In fact, it's likely going to take you quite a while to get yourself where you want to be.

Start with a single goal. After you accomplish that single goal, reward yourself. Then set a second goal, and go after it. Gradually, you will notice positive changes either in the absence of former issues or in the addition of new enhancements.

An inch less here, a pound less there. An extra block of walking, an extended glance from your spouse or an admirer. Oh, yeah!

Living Your Own Amazing Life

Now it's your turn to pause and take action. Invest a few minutes to reflect upon these questions and when you are ready, write your responses in your *Cheating Death: The 10 Thriving Life Principles Journal* or in a notebook.

1. When was the last time that you felt you were in the best shape of your life? Would it make sense to enjoy that mental, emotional, and spiritual uplift that occurs when you're in great physical health?

2. What events in your life became the excuse(s) for failing to devote enough time and attention to your healthy lifestyle?

3. What one action can you commit to undertake this week to make an incremental change in your health?

PRINCIPLE 4: FEED YOUR INTELLECT

I don't believe that our intellect or education are bounded by the societal formalities confined to classrooms. My own experience formed me from classrooms, machine shops, trenches, coffee shops, playgrounds, clubs, sports teams, home and more.

I don't believe that we are ever done learning. Gosh, I sure hope not, because I'm having too much fun continuing to learn new ideas and concepts from other people. I make mistakes in my own life and learn from those mistakes as well.

Strip away any preconceived notions that you are too smart or too dumb to continue to feed your intellect. Humble yourself and believe in yourself enough to recognize that you are both a learner and a teacher. I took a circuitous path to discover that truth for myself.

Stability Amidst Instability

From childhood I was like a shrub with shallow roots swept away by rising flood waters. I didn't recognize instability in my life, because I had a poorly developed sense of stability. Despite my lack of conscious recognition of instability, I did begin to grow toward the sunshine of hope that was academic success.

I struggled to adapt to first grade following a year of absence between pre-school and elementary school, when more transient instability during my final year in New York eliminated kindergarten as an option. I started to get the hang of the place, and began to do well in school in second grade.

Simply put, I liked the praise that I got when I answered questions correctly in class or got a one hundred percent on a spelling test. I had an insatiable thirst for reading, calculating, and learning new facts.

If I didn't have enough to keep me busy, my emotional immaturity would rear its ugly head, a weakness that would plague me into high school. In our modern world of labeling energetic children with attention deficit hyperactivity disorder (ADHD) and the like, I probably would have received such a label had they been giving them out back then.

But, for the most part, my teachers quickly learned to placate me with extra work from those enrichment modules that typically gathered dust in the classroom cupboard. By third grade I was being sent to fourth grade for math and fifth grade for English & reading.

I wasn't particularly athletic, but did manage to slip in two years of little league baseball before that slipped out of my childhood. The first year I got to pitch and play infield, and we lost every game. The second year I played on a different team, and was relegated to the outfield. We won every game, but I didn't feel the connection that I had on the no-win team.

In seventh grade, I had the good fortune to have Mrs. Elaine Edwards, the state's Teacher of the Year, as my English teacher. That year I also earned the ignoble distinction of watching my honored teacher turn beet red with furious restraint as my incessant teasing led her to call me a "snit", when she likely was trading an "h" for that "n". In eighth grade, I managed to quit the school safety patrol when I was scolded for repeatedly employing over-the-top tactics to stem what seemed like an overwhelming tide of unruly children running in the hallway.

Then, despite spending multiple days with my middle school principal Mr. George Finch in the in-school suspension room for all manner of mischief, I graduated eighth grade atop the class. Despite my teenaged ambivalence for religion mentioned in an earlier chapter, even then I began to realize that God had an ironic sense of humor. Years later as a young adult, I would develop a friendship with my former principal and have the good fortune to meet up with Mr. Finch again in Stillwater, Oklahoma for a bite to eat at Eskimo Joes.

Off to the regional high school on a forty-five minute bus ride each way for ninth grade, I continued my academic success and my intermittent sabbaticals in the in-school suspension room. All the while, I managed to make good loyal friends, attend social events, earn a few bucks doing odd jobs, and get inducted into the National Honor Society. I picked up a few social habits along the way. Then, following a particularly raucous coeducational camping outing, I also became an ex-member of a disbanded Scouting Explorer troop before graduating from a second high school fifteen hundred miles away.

Why am I sharing these events with you? Because they demonstrate how even a chaotic journey through childhood can't impede the innate intellectual ability that resides within each one of us.

The School Of Hard Knocks

My journey through higher education has become a humorous primer in later years for what *not* to do en route to earning a university degree.

I often advise middle and high school students and mentor adults aspiring to obtain a college or technical degree. I candidly tell them that if anyone can screw it up as badly as I did, and still end up earning a doctorate, then they *most surely* will be able to do it far better than me.

The only hard knocks came about because I kept striking my own hard-headed skull like a game of self-inflicted whack-a-mole.

I had it made academically when I graduated high school summa cum laude. I chose Texas A&M University as my destination two months before graduation, because my then-girlfriend was going to attend there. My National Merit Scholarship, bolstered by two additional academic scholarships, covered all of my expenses for tuition & fees, room & board, and books, leaving me with a refund.

Academically, I hit the ground running. I have always been very disciplined and well-organized when it came to academics. So I approached college like a project, developing and executing plans and tasks to achieve key milestones.

Transferring in some advanced placement credits for testing out of language arts and math, plus an insane first year pace, allowed me to earn 57 credits and a respectable GPA on the Dean's List in my first calendar year of college. Culturally, the University was a great fit for me with all of its deep traditions, engaging students, and opportunities to get involved in campus activities.

During that first summer between my freshman and sopho-more year, my inner demons began to infiltrate my otherwise smooth academic lifestyle. I had decided to remain at school to enroll in summer coursework and work. Despite my schol-arship refunds, my social life soon required more funding, so I took on three part-time jobs in addition to some campus stu-dent orientation activities.

With the additional funding, a circle of new friends, and ac-cess, I began drinking frequently and heavily at local clubs and parties. By the end of the summer, I was immersed in fraternity rush activities, purchasing trendy clothing, dining out on credit cards, and stumbling nightly into bed to nurse painful hang-overs.

Success requires routines, but the seeds of failure can be found in routines as well. And I was sowing seeds far and wide, precipi-tating a fall that I wouldn't soon forget.

Adopting a social lifestyle to which I had not previously been accustomed, my drinking and spending habits led me to take on a full-time job on nights and weekends during my sophomore year. Grades plummeted as I missed classes and commitments, sacrificing my disciplined academic approach for instant carnal gratification.

I ended my second year at University on academic probation, spent my third year haphazardly pulling myself back from the brink, before finally quitting altogether midway through my fourth year as grades, debt, and addiction pulled me under.

I had no one to blame except myself. Speaking my truth, I don't make excuses for the layers upon layers of stupidity that I had created in my attempt to be someone, something that I thought resembled a status to which I aspired.

Perhaps at some level you may even be able to relate, either personally in your own life or from the lives of others whom you've observed.

Looking back, I have no regrets for this period of time. I honestly believe that I had to cause, experience, and recover from this mess of my own making in order to fulfill my mandate to uplift others who have similarly fallen.

I would literally fall so far that I would find myself performing subterranean manual labor at a prison before I could see daylight again.

What Does It Mean To Feed Your Intellect?

Intellectual prowess need not be measured by grades, degrees, or other accolades, but should instead reflect the pursuit, mastery, and multiplying effect of that subject matter which excites your own mind. Importantly, your intellectual pursuits should not be defined or limited by narrow historical references to ivy-covered universities.

Much of the *best* intellectual work is being done in the trades, in both traditional and emerging industries. Regardless of which intellectual path you choose, know that you cannot cheat Death if you are starving your own mind. You come to love your mind for its boundless capacity to learn, retain, and improve upon new information and skills.

Although I strongly support "book learning" and the classroom experience in the formation of the intellect, I am agnostic as to what subjects those books and classes pertain, so long as you are deeping your intellect in areas of knowledge and skill for which you are deeply interested.

In other words, hearkening back to our earlier chapter

about *The Promise and the Paradox*, practicing *Principle 4* isn't about studying and mastering a subject or vocation simply because you have the aptitude for it or could earn a lot of money. That's not feeding your intellect if all you are doing is choking down dry bland morsels of knowledge at someone else's urging. No!

You feed your intellect when, after you've been exposed to a taste of something new and unfamiliar or take a fresh view of something previously overlooked, you suddenly find yourself obsessed with having to read, watch, learn, and discuss everything you can on the topic. In fact, if you just can't shut up about a subject and are drawn to others who are similarly obsessed, then you've likely developed a hunger of the soul that yearns to be fed.

Many of us sense this development in children. I make it a point to restrain myself from telling children or young adults what *I* think they should be. Instead I limit myself to encouraging them to explore what *they themselves* want to be. People have relayed memories of sleepless nights and early mornings spent pouring over every detail about horses, rockets, computers, electric guitar, woodworking, truck engines, and so on.

Perhaps you can recall when you yourself experienced this intensity in your own childhood. What turned you on?

Did you feed it until you became that which you daydreamed about? Or did other well-intentioned individuals steer you toward something a bit more...practical?

How I Came To Feed My Intellect

The principles that guide my intellectual orientation are best summed up in the phrase "Study, Immerse, and Share". This theme reflects my journey and the journey of many others, and may differ slightly or greatly from your own intellectual principles.

Study

Books.

I happened to favor books. My paternal grandparents loved books to the extent that their Brooklyn apartment had been enhanced to include several floor-to-ceiling bookshelves stuffed with every manner of book. Hardcover and paperback, every genre in print.

In addition to receiving new books as gifts from an early age, I also fondly recall that familiar aged paper scent when visiting used book stores—a pastime that my family continues to enjoy regularly. As if in the DNA that I passed to her, my daughter Elizabeth prefers a good used book, marked up on the margins, to any electronic equivalent.

Having missed Kindergarten, I struggled in first grade to catch up to grade level in reading, but by second grade had excelled to be placed a grade above for reading class. In addition to receiving extra reading assignments from school, my father made good use of our local library to load me up on biographies and other historical texts in a manner that suited our modest family budget. We would often read together.

In Miss Miller's third grade class, to keep myself out of trouble when I completed my assigned classwork early, I developed a quirky fascination with sequentially rewriting words directly out of the dictionary as I learned their definitions. The old multivolume Encyclopedia Britannica that my father owned became a favorite companion at home in a pre-internet era of youthful research. To this very day, I consume written and audio books of history and biographies with insatiable curiosity.

My studies of people, places, and events was complemented by my enjoyment of mathematics. The neatness of figures, sums, and other equations squared nicely with my search for certainty amidst my chaotic youth. The Accounting degree that I would eventually earn had its roots in this childhood pastime.

These academic disciplines converged as I settled upon business as a career choice around the age of seven, followed by my desire to pursue additional education in law that began to emerge when I was thirteen. As discussed elsewhere in this book, despite my youthful clarity about the professions for which I found alignment with my intellectual pursuits, attaining my college degree would consume twelve years before I walked across that stage.

Which brings me to an important point—books or math or classrooms don't have to be *your* preference. Many of us know women and men who are 'book smart', and yet lack common sense or street smarts. Magazines, illustrated books, comic books, audio books, and more have been created to appeal to different learning styles.

You have to identify what subject matter and style of learning turns you on intellectually. Then immerse yourself into the subject matter, and don't let anyone talk you out of it.

Immersion

When you are studying an exciting subject, time seems to stand still.

While I referenced my love of books and recounted the knowledge I gained from them, the immersion took place when I applied my knowledge and enhanced my studies with practical, hands-on experience. You aren't going to excel in your studies or your career if you stop at 'book smarts'. Even when I studied books and videos about landscaping and masonry to work on home improvement projects, the real learning literally took place when I was up to my knees in a muddy pit preparing the work site for compacted gravel.

Many of the smartest women and men I know have dirt on their faces and grease under their fingernails. The classroom forms a vital point of reference to some extent for just about any profession, but the real learning starts when you get out there in the trenches, whether figuratively or literally.

The office, the shop floor, and the job site all provide ample opportunities to immerse ourselves into our tradecraft. Often under the watchful eye of a supervisor or trainer, we venture with some uncertainty into the 'real world' to apply that which we have learned thus far.

Sometimes a veteran takes us under their wings early on, and other times we need to seek out our own mentor. Either way, the wise among us will remain humble enough to recognize and acknowledge that we know less than the more experienced women and men that preceded us.

We develop the habit of showing up early and staying late. We get to know our co-workers, our leaders, our suppliers, and our customers. We maintain our confidence in good measure. But immersion is a team sport, so pity the person who boldly strikes out on his own with self-assured cockiness, only to soil his own reputation before he's even had an opportunity to establish one.

We study everything, especially when we make the inevitable mistakes, to ensure that we move toward mastery. We exercise innovation, but we also measure twice and cut once. We get a peer or a supervisor to review our work before making decisions that, if done poorly, would needlessly result in costly, time-consuming rework.

Immersion isn't the 'you show'—it's about enhancing your own studies through hands-on application for the mutual benefit of your employer, your co-workers, your customers, and (yes) your career success. But immersion is also about the veterans who cleared the path before you to share their intellect, experience, and wisdom with you.

And then, one day the stewardship of sharing passes to you. Always be prepared, because that day will come sooner than you expected.

Sharing

Intellectual development comes full circle when you are able to share some or all that you have learned with another person. This ability unfolds incrementally and increases as you exhibit an ever greater capacity to teach others what you have mastered.

You are equipped to share intellectual gifts early in your own journey, when you sit beside a classmate or co-worker to assist them to better understand recent content. Your willingness to explain a concept or demonstrate a skill, without being asked by an instructor or supervisor to do so, will immediately build your reputation as a team player. Some women or men mistake withholding their own intellect from others as their ticket to long-term job security. But they are eventually exposed for their short-sighted selfishness and sent packing during the inevitable retooling or expense reduction that occurs.

Even before I was old enough to have working papers, I held odd jobs as a kid. Over the course of a couple summers, I picked up trash and cleared brush at a family attraction venue. Not only was I willing to come early, stay late, and cover shifts when some other kid failed to show up. I also welcomed the opportunity to show new kids how we worked. Needless to say, I got to work a lot of hours and I was fairly compensated. This experience set the tone for every job I held after that to this day.

Asking others to share what they knew better than I did, as well as sharing what I knew with others only led to favorable outcomes. I've trained, coached, mentored, and championed women and men throughout my career. I've provided guidance from the boardroom and the C-suite. While I've developed many leaders across multiple disciplines, and received promotions and financial abundance in return, I have never experienced a financial set-back or occupational layoff as a result of my willingness to share what I could.

Intellectual ability is an asset that, once gained, becomes a stewardship for which we are entrusted to give freely to those who seek opportunities to advance and are committed to applying themselves diligently to the effort. Share your knowledge and experience generously with others.

Taking Action: Feeding Your Intellect To Win Your Amazing Life

Feeding your intellect begins with you. You've already demonstrated that you are intelligent by picking up this book and challenging yourself to live a more amazing life. You've further demonstrated that you're smart by being good at many skills in your life, both personally and professionally.

Graduating from school wasn't the end of the intellectual road, but merely a stage that prepared you for the career into which you entered. I'm challenging you to go farther and regenerate a part of you that yearns to be fed a rich diet of tantalizing information and practical skills. There are no limits to how much you can learn.

If you've already mastered your career, and yet you know that your mind and soul yearn for more intellectual nourishment, then stop limiting yourself to the same old magazines, training classes, and professional conferences. Sure, you may still want to stay on top of any new developments and maintain strong camaraderie with you colleagues, but you don't have to pretend that there isn't a frontier of knowledge beyond that job.

You've likely set aside some of those obsessions, those passions that kept you awake at night as child or young adult. True, some of them may no longer be practical. Perhaps you're not going to play for your favorite professional sports team. But at least one or more of your youthful passions may remain relevant to you to this very day. Or maybe you have to go sample from the buffet of life and identify new topics.

Either way, the first step to taking action to feed your intellect is to pick something that moves you, and then get moving. And if the first thing that you decide to learn more about doesn't hold your interest as much as it did twenty-five years ago, then try the next thing.

Buy or borrow a book. Join a club. Take a class. Attend a lecture. Read a blog. Watch a video. There is no wrong way to feed your intellect. Enjoy the process as you study and immerse yourself into your intellectual pursuit. Engage in this intellectual journey with a friend or group. Share what you are learning with loved ones and trusted friends.

I'm not suggesting that every intellectual avenue will lead you away from your career into some new artistic or entrepreneurial endeavor. You might already own your business or love the career at which you excel. But I've never met a woman or man who isn't more fulfilled and enjoying a more amazing life once the appetite for additional intellectual delights is unleashed.

I've also encountered more than a few individuals who've uncovered passions that subsequently revealed themselves to be more attractive than the vocation to which she or he had devoted two or three decades. And that's okay, too.

Sometimes we take off the suit and put on the smock. Sometimes we take off the smock and put on the suit. It's your life and you're still alive, so don't be surprised when feeding your intellect blossoms into amazing ventures as yet unconceived.

I can't wait to hear about your experiences feeding your intellect.

Living Your Own Amazing Life

Now it's your turn to pause and take action. Invest a few minutes to reflect upon these questions and when you are ready, write your responses in your *Cheating Death: The 10 Thriving Life Principles Journal* or in a notebook.

1. What mental obsessions and passions filled your daydreams and kept you awake at night as a child or young adult? What caused you to lay them aside?

2. As you reflect on your current intellectual and vocational interests, what is one topic that you would like to learn more about now?

3. What one action can you take tomorrow to begin your journey to feed your intellect on that topic?

PRINCIPLE 5: EMBRACE EMOTIONAL BLISS

*"Running is about finding your inner peace,
and so is a life well lived."*

~ DEAN KARNAZES[11]

A s my beautiful bride could confirm from our earliest days, I was an emotional hot mess when she met me.

Looking backward in time, I can recognize the impact that various well-intentioned role models had on my emotional development. Parents and step-parents whom I love deeply to this day were unfortunately ill-equipped decades ago, still in their own developmental youth to one degree or another, to prepare me adequately for the world. They loved me then as they love me now, but they simply didn't know what they didn't know. As a child and teenager, I also did not have a foundation in emotional stability to offer.

As I discussed at the beginning of *Principle 1: Speak Your Truth*, my childhood memories were formed amidst emotional coldness, immaturity, and arguments that led to marital and geographical separation. As a result, I grew up exhibiting emotional extremes that didn't square well with my own self-concept nor with forming healthy relationships with others. Sure, I made lifelong friends and got along reasonably well with people. But I carried so much emotional baggage into my teen years that I should have either summoned a bellhop or a psychologist to extract me from myself.

Winds Of Change

No such luck at finding anyone to relieve me of my teenaged angst or emotional baggage. Instead, I simply got tired of chasing after nothing. I got tired of fighting with my father and stepmother at the top of my lungs. I got tired of feeling like I didn't fit in.

So, at fifteen years old, not particularly constrained by any one group of friends, activity, or family structure, I did the only thing that came naturally to me. No roots, no problem. I said my good-byes, packed my bags, and made arrangements to move halfway across the country from New England to Houston.

I had traveled to Houston several times previously to visit my mother and cousins. The lure of the warmer weather, the welcoming friendliness of the strangers I met, and my yearning for a fresh start all intermingled to draw me there following my tenth grade in high school.

Beginning my junior year at a new school in the Lone Star state was significantly eased by my summertime introduction to several students on the cross country team. I had yearned to participate in cross country and other sports earlier in high school, but family circumstances had prevented me from realizing my desire. In fact, joining cross country had been one of the pillars to substantiate my departure from my former home, a fact that likely appeared frivolously angsty to my father and stepmother.

Running. It became the perfect metaphor for transitioning from my old life to my new life. But I truly had loved running for many years. As detailed in a prior chapter, I was (and still am) built for distance running, and the feeling of freedom that comes with lacing up and going wherever one's heart, mind, and soul leads me has an irreplaceable appeal.

Coach Andy Ferrara and my fellow teammates were very welcoming, and became lifelong friends of mine. While I certainly wasn't the fastest runner on the team, the sense of belonging pushed me to train harder and compete with a joyful intensity that helped to shake the dust of my past off of me to some extent. Earning my varsity letter replaced the imaginary scarlet letter of solitude that had previously burned shamefully in my imagination.

My youthful emotional experience didn't crush any dreams nor kill my spirit. Quite the opposite, it inspired me to never stop tilling the ground, planting the seeds, and believing that the inevitable downpours life cast upon me would one day deliver me to help myself and help others.

Life had truly only just begun. It would take me well into my adulthood to discover and consistently enjoy emotional bliss. Along the way I damaged myself and others, for which I have made my amends.

What Does It Mean To Embrace Emotional Bliss?

Emotional bliss is that state of personal emotional health that allows you to function day in, day out, from a foundation of stability. Since each of us is wired differently as a result of our childhood role models, experiences, and relationships, emotional health will develop and manifest itself uniquely within each of us. The common element is the foundation of stability, because no matter where we begin our journey toward emotional bliss, the finish line is essentially the same. Peace of mind and enjoyment of this amazing life in all of its ups and downs at whatever level we can handle. You come to love yourself and others regardless of the emotional ups and downs, past, present or future.

I don't believe in the myth of the perfect childhood, perfect parents, or perfect emotional formation. That's not to say that you may not have lived a fantastic childhood with phenomenal loving parents who provided you a solid emotional upbringing. I'm just suggesting that we have all hit a few bumps in the road throughout our lives that have delivered some emotional bruises and quite possibly, some emotional scars. If you allow those emotional bruises to burst and fester as open wounds, you will surely not be able to cheat Death.

Emotional bliss isn't a synthetic euphoric state that enables you to glide through life immune to heartbreaks, anger, and disappointment. Nor is emotional bliss emblematic of a false permanent state of rah-rah motivation that you can turn on at a moment's notice to project to the world. No, in fact, emotional bliss provides that foundation of stability to which you can return, in moments or over the course of time, when life events catch you off guard. But because you will have developed that foundation, you will always be confident that there is somewhere solid and safe within yourself to return.

Emotional bliss is about your inner peace and love. You don't have to put on an act for yourself or anyone else around you. When you're happy, you don't need to apologize for it just because someone else isn't feeling happy. When you're sad, you don't need to put on a "happy face" and pretend for your family or your co-workers that "everything is fine".

Sometimes you aren't feeling fine inside, and that is perfectly normal. You are human—not artificial intelligence—and thus blessed with the full array of emotions, even those that you're not quite sure what triggered them and can't always dispense with quickly.

In fact, sometimes you are comfortable sharing your emotions with loved ones, while at other times you may frankly require community or professional help. Never hesitate to take whatever action is necessary to embrace emotional bliss and fully live your amazing life.

As with each of these principles, I don't have *Principle 5* entirely figured out myself. Yes, I'm still strengthening my own emotional foundation after all these years. But I'll assure you, even with the extent of emotional bliss that I have come to experience in my life, and the peace of mind that I've seen cascade over other women and men, I wouldn't trade the fractured journey to get here for all the world. As we'll discuss in the next section, the journey requires some good honest reflection and patience. You are well worth it!

How I Came To Embrace Emotional Bliss

The tenets that guide my emotional presence are best summed up in the phrase "Healing, Baseline, and Love". This trajectory reflects my own exploratory path and is evident in the many women and men whom I visit with, and yet may differ slightly or greatly from your own unique and special emotional journey.

Healing

I believe that the pathway to fully embracing your emotional bliss begins with healing and loving yourself.

I truly didn't understand the power of healing in my own life until my journey was well underway. I had become numb to the chronic emotional pain that had begun in my childhood and seemed to characterize many interludes in my life. I tasted bitterness in every memory and infused every new potential relationship with its filthy residue.

I did not consciously recognize that my own brokenness was the *source* of the interpersonal conflicts that I had taken into young adulthood with me. Because I could rationalize the reason why relationships—romantic, professional, community—ended, sometimes abruptly, I had come to instinctually remove emotion from many painful situations. When I did bring emotion to the situation, it was often misaligned and outsized for what would have been more appropriate.

But as I was getting older, I did begin to notice uncomfortable and embarrassing patterns emerging from situations that appeared to repeat themselves. Dating relationships and job changes were two areas that were initially easy to justify for seemingly *logical* reasons, but upon further introspection became areas of concern for me.

I wasn't getting any younger and I appeared to be repeating the same lack of emotional skill over and over again. If I had been seeking to launch a career in stand-up comedy, my script could have provided fodder for my darkly humorous routine.

It's one thing to be engaging in new relationships and new jobs at an early time when roots may not have yet been set down. But as the years tolled on, I wasn't able to sustain a healthy relationship with the intelligent beautiful women that were attracted to me, or progress professionally with certain styles of bosses. When I did succeed in new relationships, it was in spite of my own emotional misconstruction.

Guided by my inner grit that has always led me like a beacon in the fog to find a way to self-improvement, I knew that I had to change my ways. I didn't yet know exactly what "my ways" were, but I knew the symptoms and the aftermath that resulted.

I was alone even when I was with others, and it was deepening my inner sorrow. I absolutely had to change, and so began my earnest search for emotional bliss.

As I mentioned in the prior chapter (*Principle 4: Feed Your Intellect*), I love to read, so I read voraciously about any topic that helped to explain feelings, habits, and social dynamics. Psychology, leadership, communication. You name it, and I was reading it. I camped out in public libraries, chain bookstores, and coffee shops, hunkered down with every pertinent book I could get my hands on.

There was no lightbulb moment when it all just came together and I embraced emotional bliss, closed the book, and stepped into the perfect dating relationship and perfect professional relationship. I'd like to be able to tell you that I found the solution in one particular chapter or one entire book, but in fact the books were more like meals that provided sustenance for a much longer journey. Into myself. The healing had begun.

I couldn't simply check out of life, figure it all out, and then re-engage with society as an emotionally perfect being. Instead, I read, journaled, talked to friends and family, observed myself, and retooled in-flight. I did become very comfortable with my complex past, exploring and drawing comprehension from the innumerable events that had influenced my emotional profile from early childhood to the present.

Importantly, I took ownership of the many ways in which my emotional deficiencies had caused my own pain and had negatively impacted others. I was the problem, and I remained accountable for my past.

As an introspective individual, I employed my tendency to ponder and examine events to take hold of my healing process. If something transpired such that the outcome was less than optimal, I would mull it over and then look for similar past instances in the pattern. I would replay the recent event in slow motion in my mind, seeking to identify the moment where I allowed my emotions to veer off course. I was troubleshooting my own errors to reengineer my emotional shortcomings.

I began to get better at identifying the triggers that unearthed historical fears and pain. While I couldn't go back and repair each incident that I caused, I did make it a point to circle back and give explanation and apology where it was both possible and appropriate. I went further back into my life, seeking people out to make amends. Where I couldn't make amends *directly* due to preventative or permanently changed circumstances, I would write out or speak my amends toward that individual and offer them up as a prayer.

In addition to making amends where I had caused emotional pain, I accepted and forgave others who had caused me pain. I recalled incidents or extended situations that had impacted me. I did not generally seek out the participants, who were often at a distance or no longer alive. Instead, I wrote about the situations and the people involved, sometimes as narratives, and sometimes as mock dialogues. The point was to acknowledge visibly the life events that had inflicted the pain that continued to mar my adult emotional framework, and then to move on from those events without the residual downside effects.

As the emotional baggage of past hurts and self-denied pain continued to dissipate, my emotional "muscles" strengthened. While I won't go so far as to say that there couldn't be some past hurt or entrenched emotional pain hidden in my psyche yet to be dislodged, I cannot consciously recall any that remain. I simply seek not to repeat past emotional outbursts nor create new emotional rifts. In a non-clinical way, I reached a point somewhere along the journey where I felt emotionally healthy. I had reached my baseline, no longer feeling broken and ashamed.

Baseline

My idea of the "emotional baseline" will be different for you than it is for me or for any other individual. Starting from where I had begun emotionally to subsequently achieve self-aware-ness of my negative tendencies and patterns, my experience to reach my baseline wasn't marked by a single point in time. I would consider myself to continually be improving the base-line even to this day.

Early on in my emotional recovery, reaching some level of baseline was both a daily challenge and a daily victory. It may have been as simple as not allowing the commonplace annoy-ances of delays, misunderstandings, or miscommunication to trigger me to say something inappropriate or hurtful.

Associating longer term negative consequences with short term outbursts guided me to avoid giving voice to the thoughts that arose in my head. Instead, I developed a habit of imagining thought bubbles capturing what I would have liked to say, and painlessly carrying those snarky ideas off into the ether. That process continues to humor me to this day, and helps me to ensure that I'm not needlessly offending others when circum-stances or situations frustrate me.

For me the emotional baseline is simply that highest level of normalcy that I can maintain throughout the day in every moment, whether I am alone or engaged with others, to be at peace with myself. While seemingly second nature and often on autopilot, I none the less remain attuned to my own emotions throughout the day, checking myself to ensure that I remain well-balanced.

What has resulted over time is that the baseline has become the default condition. Because I long ago brought the po-tentially devastating effects of emotional pain under control through healing, I do not worry about devolving into extended negative emotional states. Instead, the balance in my emotional surplus has continued to amass over these many years to overflowing. Though it began gradually at first, my need to love both myself and others has intensified to where I find myself at this point in my life.

Love

In my life, love has not been an event or a series of relationships. Love has been a constant energy source that has always been present in my life. Despite the challenges that I have noted elsewhere, I know without a doubt that my parents, stepmother, and extended family loved me dearly as a child. I have also loved, and been loved by friends, family members and romantic partners—especially my beautiful bride—throughout my life.

Love was the source of the healing that I undertook to recognize, reconcile, and remove the emotional pain from my life. Love was the touchstone that guided me to identify, strengthen, and consistently operate from a baseline of healthy emotions.

But the truly unexpected benefit of healing and then adhering to a baseline of healthy emotions was the increasing abundance of love that swelled in my life. The more love I felt for myself, the more I had to give love away. I had to express love in my home, in the workplace, in my casual interactions with strangers whom I'd encounter in daily living.

Though I'm sure I caused more than one awkward interaction, for the most part I was often giving love away without anyone knowing what I was doing. Truth be told, in the beginning I wasn't entirely sure what I was doing. It started out as smiles, kind words, acknowledgement for something well done. It grew into a daily habit of good-finding to where I am now in the present moments of my life. I was created by God to love.

I love myself with self-respect and dignity, granting myself the grace to be imperfect. At home, my love for my beautiful bride Kimberly and my amazing daughter Elizabeth burns brightly and grows daily. Extended family and friends are a delight, and I seek them out for laughter and extend a hand of hope when they are hurting. I feel love for the teams that I lead and those of which I am a member.

In our community and in all communities that I visit, I capture the goodness that I observe in each individual whom I encounter, whether directly or indirectly, and I pour out the love of our human interconnectedness as it has been so generously poured out onto me. I love strangers and I love the women and men who I have yet to meet.

I am not naïve. Life isn't always a love fest and my perspective isn't always mutually felt. But I take a long-term view of relationships in this ever-shortening life that remains for me. So I try not to jump to conclusions.

Some people act with clumsy or immature intentions that bring hurt to a new or established relationship. Heck, that would have accurately described me in my youth and young adulthood. While it is easy to pass off the rude stranger as I will likely never encounter them again, the family member or colleague who visits emotional pain on me is someone with whom I will wish to reconcile.

Initially, I figure that everyone has a bad day sometime, and if the slight does not recur on a future visit, then I can lay it to rest. Where the emotional pain persists in future interactions, I seek to calmly address it directly. I may not always remain calm, but I strive to be.

I have found that most people are acting out, often unknowingly, from an underlying cause of their own personal frustration. When brought to their attention in a spirit of non-judgmental love, they can speak more openly about their own fears, concerns, pain. While I may not have the ready solution to their situation, my very exercise of genuine loving concern has often applied the balm that was needed. At other times, I encounter some people who are so immersed in their self-loathing that no amount of my love will resolve their issues for the moment.

I don't have emotional bliss all figured out. Sometimes I will require healing for reasons that I am not entirely certain, perhaps something as simple as a troubling dream that causes me to wake up on the wrong side of the bed. My initial objective is always to return to the steady state of emotional balance upon which all other facets of my life rely. But then having easily regained my balance, I set off immediately to dish out a daily dose of love to all whom I encounter.

My life is like a team sport well played, and of which I never tire. At the end of each day, I look back with a clean conscience. If I have offended anyone, I take comfort knowing that I either took care to restore love in the moment or will at its next opportunity. I acknowledge that I am an imperfect human being seeking to live this most amazing life.

But even more importantly, I fall into bed confident that I have given all the surplus love that I had to give that day, and excited that I will awake the next morning (God willing!) with even more abundant love to freely share.

Taking Action: Embracing Emotional Bliss To Win Your Amazing Life

At this point, you can safely assume that if someone as messed up as I was could eventually grow to embrace emotional bliss and live an amazing life, then you *most certainly* can do it. You're likely in a much better state emotionally today than I was when I hit rock bottom.

As with each of *The 10 Thriving Life Principles*, *Principle 5* requires you to begin at the beginning. The beginning is healing, and you can take as long as you need to heal. Embracing emotional bliss is aspirational yet achievable, so there is no sense in placing artificial timelines that create undue pressure to get it all figured out by some fixed point in time.

Simply be.

Be angry.

Be sad.

Be disappointed.

Be embarrassed.

Be remorseful.

And so forth.

Take as long as you need to take to reflect on all the past incidents and the pain associated with them. I recommend writing them down, not so that you can go back and relive or reread them, but so that you can draw these memories out of your mind, heart and soul. Once recorded in your *Cheating Death: The 10 Thriving Life Principles Journal* or in a notebook, you can spend all the time you need feeling the uncomfortable emotions before moving on.

No matter how dark your past was, your future need not repeat that past. You can take a red pen or a black marker and cross through or entirely blot out those painful memories in your *Journal*.

You didn't write them for anyone else except you.

You didn't write them to relive them, but to *release* them.

Whether you believe that you are due amends, or that you

owe amends to someone, you may choose the method that suits your healing best.

You might decide to write a letter to that person, place it in an envelope, and set it in a drawer or box for safekeeping, with no intention whatsoever to send it. By your very act of writing the letter with that individual firmly in your mind, you have expressed the positive emotions that release you from the past hurt. This method works particularly well when reconciling emotions with those individuals who have passed away or for whom actual contact would be ill-advised or unnecessarily disruptive, as in the case of an ex-spouse who has remarried or an abuser who has been released from incarceration.

In other instances, you may choose an in-person gathering or telephone call to have a heart-to-heart talk with someone you hurt or who hurt you. In the case of your spouse, life partner, parent, or child, I have found that in-person discussions are generally the best scenario. You have to do what works best for you.

Healing isn't always a balanced equation. While you may be seeking to deliver or to receive an apology, understand in advance that all you can control is your side of the discussion. Whether you are making amends for your own actions, or you are seeking to clear the air for something that you perceive was done to you, you cannot guarantee that the other individual will view the past situation the same way or be prepared to offer the response that you desire.

I encourage you to be comfortable embarking on your healing path confident that each step forward, no matter how difficult, how slowly, how painfully, none the less represents real progress toward your emotional bliss. We grow as we go.

Principle 5 isn't linear. Even as you progress in your healing and achieve a modicum of daily baseline, you will find yourself requiring more healing. Similarly, since you're already engaged in relationships with other individuals as you embark on your healing path, you will be giving love where others are worthy of your love. And you certainly should be giving love to your-self daily. Thus, there is no one right way to embrace emotional bliss—there is only *your* way.

Achieving a baseline in your life may actually be uncom-fortable. At least I found it to be uncomfortable at first. The emotional stability, no matter how fleeting at first, that an emotional baseline provides can almost seem like an un-deserved gift if you had become accustomed to years (or dec-ades) of emotional upheaval. When the gusts stop blowing and the whitecaps settle down, some individuals have told me that they had difficulty getting their footing on a deck that no longer undulated wildly. Let's face it—emotional chaos is its own spe-cial brand of daily excitement, no matter how twisted that sounds in retrospect!

In the beginning of reclaiming your amazing life when embra-cing emotional bliss, you may only be able to achieve baseline for hours at a time. In fact, while you may achieve it at home in the morning, baseline might succumb to chaos the moment you get stuck in rush hour traffic on the way to work and the frustra-tions of the day take over.

Slipping back into the emotional muck is normal. Don't fret and don't you even dare think of giving in. Take a daily inven-tory. Make the amends you can. And start the next day all over again.

Like any new habit, it takes time, patience, and grace. Give yourself a limitless runway to keep moving forward, healing a little more each day, and extending your baseline from minutes to hours to days over the course of time. As long as it takes. It's *your* life!

What's Love Got To Do With It?

Everything.

Love is the fuel that permeates each of *The 10 Thriving Life Principles*, and embracing your emotional bliss is certainly at the heart of your amazing life. At this early stage of your journey, you may not be feeling the love. And that's ok.

You may also not be ready to give love, and that's perfectly ok as well.

But when you have but one ounce of love to give, be sure that you give it to yourself first. Much like the familiar pre-flight guidance on commercial airlines, be sure to secure your own oxygen mask before assisting others with their masks. Your cup must first be filled with a sustainable level of love before you can be expected to share true love with others.

This may sound like a contradiction to what I mentioned a few minutes ago, but I'm talking first about sustainability. It is then true that once you have love in your cup then you should seek to share as much love with others as you are capable of sharing. But I am emphasizing that you cannot give what you yourself do not yet feel in your own heart and soul.

Oh, happy day! When you do find yourself able to share love with others, perhaps even just a little smile here or a kind word there, you immediately begin to feel the love bouncing back to you. Genuine smiles are met with genuine smiles. Kind words beget kind words. Selfless actions to help another are returned with appreciative thanks.

It's not that you're giving love to get love. But it just happens to work out that way as a natural human instinct. Love is just the gift that keeps on giving and giving and giving. Or as my cousin Regina would say, good vibes!

So, where does that lead you? As I mentioned a few minutes ago, I myself am still on this journey. I have healed, achieved a stable baseline, and express abundant love. But I am also a flawed human being, so I also still screw it up nearly daily. An unkind word to a loved one. An unkind action toward a stranger. I catch myself more often than not, and make my amends in real-time or nearly so. As a backstop, I take my own inventory and make my amends at the next opportunity.

My point is, you are already on the path to embracing your emotional bliss, simply because you've demonstrated a willingness to do so. You may not yet notice it. Perhaps no one else may notice a change in you right away. But I notice it, because I know that you—like the many women and men who have begun the journey before you— are committed to fully living your amazing life with the people you love.

How let's pause for as long as you need, so that you can take some actions to begin to embrace your emotional bliss.

Living Your Own Amazing Life

Now it's your turn to pause and take action. Invest a few minutes to reflect upon these questions and when you are ready, write your responses in your *Cheating Death: The 10 Thriving Life Principles Journal* or in a notebook.

1. Picture a person who caused you significant emotional damage in your life, and recall the event(s) that embedded that pain within your soul. If you were to seek to release that pain from your being, what method might you choose to do so?

2. Choose a person whom you hurt in your past (it could be long

ago or recently). If you were to seek to make amends with that individual, how might you choose to do so?

3. What is one new action that you can take each day, beginning today, to demonstrate genuine love for yourself?

PRINCIPLE 6: CHERISH YOUR FAMILY

*"To us, family means putting your arms around each
other and being there. No family is perfect, and
no family is without pain and suffering."*

~ BARBARA BUSH[12]

Studying and applying *Principle 5*, we come to recognize that living an amazing life is predicated on embracing our emotional bliss. When you love yourself, love other women and men, and allow yourself to receive love from others, big things happen and your life is forever changed. You have likely noticed that love (beyond yourself) involves other people.

Although I've made nearly every mistake when it comes to family that a man might make, I am humbled daily by the boundless blessing that my own family is to me. As I was deficient in *The 10 Thriving Life Principles* well into adulthood, I did not meet my beautiful bride Kimberly until my late twenties when we were both attending night school at Johnson & Wales University in Providence, Rhode Island. My life was forever changed for the better.

A few years after we married, Kimberly and I were blessed to bring Elizabeth into the world. I've been wrapped around my daughter's finger ever since the day she was born. The joy and pride that she brings to Kimberly and me is unsurpassed by any milestone or accomplishment in the material world. Our home radiates with the love that only God can bring to the imperfection that is family. I say imperfection, because just like your own home where you've raised your family, we also bicker and argue at times as we express our intergenerational viewpoints. Wouldn't trade my family for all the fame and fortune imaginable.

I have always held a broad view of family. My view of family finds support in my faith, where Jesus often ate meals with people whom he had never personally encountered before. Sometimes they were wealthy, powerful members of the elite. At other times, they were the poor, the physically challenged, the outcasts, and the homeless. We are all broken spiritually in some manner.

Now, we all know that I'm certainly not Jesus. But I am astute enough to understand that what Jesus was modeling for me was an attitude of nonjudgmental love when it came to welcoming other folks into a relationship of communion. One big happy family.

I was raised by loving parents and extended families who did the best they could with the skills, emotions, and resources that they had. I learned many lessons about family life as I grew up. Some of those lessons remain at the foundation of how I cherish my own family today. Other lessons had to be excised for the cancerous relationship tumors that they had grotesquely grown to be. All told, I have developed even stronger loving bonds with my parents, siblings and extended families that sustain me to this day.

Choose Life

I have come to believe that family life is best when it is fully lived and enjoyed. I reached this conclusion over the course of many years as I observed all manner of family living in myself and others. I have chosen a somewhat unconventional mode of living that prioritizes the quality time I spend with my family members and friends over societal expectations of administering the household.

While I agree that most families are committed to quality time, I had also come to realize that many families invest far too much time in keeping up appearances, going through the motions, and spending time doing stuff that really won't matter in the long run.

The Cleanest Home myth

Into her seventies, my mother has maintained a daily devotion to neatness and orderliness. Vacuumed carpets, clean dishes, folded laundry, and perfectly aligned fringe are hallmarks of a good day in my mother's life. But I also listened to her frustration about the never-ending list of tasks, many of them recurring, and how she 'didn't have enough time to do things to care for herself'.

I admit that her influence stayed with me well into my adult life. As a young bachelor, I cycled through a checklist of chores to ensure that I fulfilled the family traditions in my own home. As a married homeowner in the early days, I would lead our charge each weekend to tidy up and clean rooms one by one.

Even when our daughter Elizabeth was younger, I sought to retain these habits as if they were the oxygen of adulthood. But as opportunities to play games together, create crafts, and engage in family trips to zoos, museums, and athletic events multiplied, I gradually came to realize that our lives weren't buried in the literal dust that sometimes began to accumulate on the coffee table.

We didn't devolve into filthy animals whose home reeked of rotting food and putrid laundry. But despite adhering to the cleaning checklist I had inherited and followed since I went away to college, I had to concede that I hadn't yet won any awards for maintaining the cleanest house on the block, and wasn't likely to any time soon. Acceptance set in. Choices became even easier.

Even more striking was that we rarely got sick, and certainly far less than the people we knew who were diving into weekly house cleaning rituals. Countertops got sanitized, dishes were cleaned, and clothing was washed, dried, and put away. COVID-19 did not take up residence in our home when the pandemic encircled the globe.

Eventually, deep cleaning took on the prioritization of an occasional pre-holiday project where tasks could get chunked together and made into something of a family "game" with the promise of more leisurely fun once the necessary items were completed. Similarly, when family would be coming to stay with us for a visit, we were able to muster ourselves to put the house back in order.

But as we threw ourselves headfirst into coaching and attending youth sporting events, artistic pursuits in theatre and music, and travel, we quickly realized that our home wasn't being raided by the Cleanliness Police. Lifelong memories were being made amidst laughter, and our adulthood hadn't been revoked.

We came to understand with a real-world perspective that the societal obsession with the perfectly clean house is truly a myth. I could live with the dust, the spot on the kitchen floor, the small pile of dishes in the kitchen sink. But I never could have accepted that I'd miss an invitation to go play golf with my amazing daughter or a trip to the gym with my bride.

The Leaf-Free Yard myth

Oh, but it didn't stop inside the home. We took this myth-busting outside and put it on full display for the entire neighborhood.

Everyone has that neighbor. If you live in a snow zone, she's the one who shovels the snow when the first flake appears and then comes out every thirty minutes for the duration of the snowfall to maintain a flake-free sidewalk and porch, as if the coating were nature's graffiti on her perfect property.

Or the guy who washes his car between rain showers when the temperature is just above the freezing point, or mows his grass despite the downpour. Generally, I see people doing this as I walk or drive around town, and they often appear to me as if they execute these tasks on a set schedule every week irrespective of weather conditions.

The final straw for me was leaf raking. I observe with a special fascination the folks who rake every last leaf between their property lines, filling dozens of those paper lawn bags, without any thought given to the impending windy weather that is going to shift every neighboring yard's leaves onto their own property before they've awoken the following day.

I recall one particular year, when I watched as homeowner after homeowner raked and bagged, raked and bagged, only to be beset by several inches of snow the following day. I had already raked and mulched earlier in the season, so my remaining leaves (blown from neighboring yards thereafter) had lain dormant as the snow blanketed our yard. Melting took several days, whereafter the leaves were much more compact and further along on their way to decomposition. So I did absolutely nothing further to remove them, figuring that they would disintegrate into the soil by springtime.

But, lo and behold, within hours of the final melting some days later, homeowners galore were back out in full force raking and bagging, raking and bagging—many doing so in the late autumn darkness that plagues us after daylight savings time goes into effect.

The leaves in my yard will eventually decompose into the earth, as will I. Better that they be left largely to their own demise, and that I and my family should live this amazing life as fully as we are capable, than for me to waste my time trying to beat foliage and wind at their own infinite game.

As far as the snow, it gets shoveled reasonably well at my house, as does the grass get mowed often enough to avoid confusion with the savannah. Admittedly, I've never been a fan of washing our own vehicles. I have determined that a minimal investment in an automated car wash, a bottle of window cleaner, and a moist dust cloth are sufficient to maintain the reasonable appearance of our vehicles. After all, it's a mode of transportation, not a museum.

As I and my family set off for the gym, or dinner, or music lessons, I can't help but smile smugly to myself. I choose life with my family, thoroughly enjoying the time that we have to spend together. At some point in the future, my daughter will move away. We won't get to recapture the moments of participating in youthful activities together. Why would I want to waste those quality family moments with rake and wash bucket in hand?

I have grown to harbor no doubts that it's far better to invest our time into cherishing our loved ones than into upholding the myths of the Cleanest Home or the perfect Leaf-Free Yard.

What Does It Mean To Cherish Your Family?

In a society increasingly driven by metrics, *Principle 6* is countercyclical. There is no universal measurement that is going to tell you or anyone else how well you're doing with this principle.

Cherishing your family is purely centered on developing and strengthening relationships with the people that you love. And like oxygen, cherishing your family is a daily requirement. But taking your family for granted, failing to nurture and demonstrate your genuine love for each member, is precisely the asphyxiation that will prevent you from cheating Death. You come to love your family as deeply and readily as if your love for them under any and all circumstances were literally the oxygen required for life.

Your family is comprised of you and any other human or living being whom you love so much that you will invest all of your spiritual, emotional, chronological, and industrial energy into them to ensure that they feel your love in the depths of their soul. It all begins with you, and that is why *Principle 6* follows the earlier principles. Absent some progress and maintenance of our spiritual, physical, and emotional foundation, we remain ill-equipped ourselves to be able to truly love another person in our family circle.

How we choose to express our love for others is unique to our relationship with that woman, man, or child. We express our love differently within the context of each relationship, ensuring that mutual, consensual, and moral considerations always govern our words and actions.

The love we share with our spouse or partner differs greatly from the love that we share with our children or our siblings. But like the rainbow of colors available to us in a grand palette, each shade of love is vital and necessary to the family master-piece that we are endowed to create.

That being said, love is powerful and should not be subjected to anachronistic boundaries or politically-correct limitations designed to substitute the judgment of scared and shrunken hearts and minds for the pure emotion that resonates within and between you and another adult human being.

I have long held a broad and scalable conception of family. If you are a friend, a client, a colleague, or related to me by blood or marriage, then we're family. In an extended fashion, you may include your domesticated pets within your family con-cept. And, yes, I believe that your pets are beloved family mem-bers—I know that ours sure are!

Being family implies that I'm going to care about you and be there for you to the extent that I can be. Being family doesn't necessarily mean that we'll have a perfect relationship every minute of the day, but it does mean that I'll do my best and I trust that you'll do your best.

Families aren't perfect, because they are comprised of imper-fect human beings. But we look for something to cherish in each woman or man we encounter, and allow the relationship to build from there. But oftentimes, we complicate our family bonds by allowing distractions to get in the way that then re-quire us to regain our focus on the priority of simply loving and cherishing those individuals to whom we have committed our entire selves.

How I Came To Cherish My Family

When it comes to living *The 10 Thriving Life Principles*, I am constantly reminded that I don't have it all figured out yet. I came to cherish my family on the journey of lessons learned from my failures involving relationships with women and men since childhood. My beautiful bride Kimberly knows that I'm not perfect, as does my amazing daughter Elizabeth. They've never demanded perfection from me, though I aspirationally will strive to cherish them to that standard my entire life.

Living a principle-centered life has many advantages, not the least of which often involves becoming part of an amazing family. I have come to cherish and deeply love my family on so many levels, from my parents and extended family to my own immediate household. The "stay home, stay safe" interlude brought about by the COVID-19 public health situation was a blessing to our family as we worked on school and career under one roof. Eating lunch together, making puzzles, and playing games represented dividends of unexpected togetherness that we could not have envisioned only weeks prior.

While my own childhood had its ups and downs, I also came to learn as a parent that children don't come with an instruction manual. Like my own parents, I was going to end up doing the best that I could with the knowledge and experience that I had gained. I am blessed to have a stellar parenting partner in my beautiful bride.

Stalking My Wife

At this point, you may be thinking, *"Cris, now you've gone too far!"*

But as I discussed in conjunction with *Principle 5*, my lack of mastery over my emotions for much of my youth and young adulthood led to me failing to form healthy relationships. While dating was never in short supply, the toxicity that I brought to many of those earlier encounters turned even the most promising relationships into train wrecks for many years.

Candidly, Kimberly—the loving and patient woman who would become my beautiful bride in 2001—would concede that I still required emotional growth long after we met. That's the wonderful truth about living *The 10 Thriving Life Principles*. You and I don't have to first *master* them to practice and improve upon them in our own amazing lives. Instead, it's an "on-the-job" experience that allows me to continue to this very day to practice and improve upon how I understand and exemplify the principles as I live my most amazing life.

One of the blessings of having spent twelve years earning an undergraduate university degree, is that I found myself enrolled in night school at Johnson & Wales University in Providence, Rhode Island in the fall of 1997. It was there that I had the good fortune of meeting Kimberly during the mid-evening breaks, which a group of us students shared together at an on-campus cafe.

I don't recall every detail of those early weeks getting to know each other, but the turning point came when I had learned that Kimberly walked home each night from class at 10 p.m. through a questionable neighborhood to her walk-up flat. I had seen her walking one night as I went to my truck, so I offered her a ride in my dented 1993 red pickup truck, which she politely refused.

So, I did what I thought any chivalrous young man would do. I told her that she could either accept my offer of a ride, or I would simply drive in the street beside where she walked on the sidewalk for the entire couple miles home. She relented, because one of our fellow students, Angela, was there to observe the exchange and vouch for my character. Kimberly figured that if she came up missing, at least there would be a witness to the crime.

Kimberly made it home without incident from that ride. When she told her roommates the story, they dubbed me her "stalker". We began dating about a month later, after Kimberly returned from Michigan where she had celebrated the Christmas holiday with her family. Even that trip home led to another funny incident, when her brother Mark exclaimed, "You're not dating any twenty-nine year old!", in light of the fact that she was nine years my junior. We still laugh about that when we relay these stories to others, and Mark became the best brother-in-law that a guy could have.

I am so fortunate that I met Kimberly during that brief window of night school, because I graduated the following spring, after which I entered law school at an entirely different university. Amidst us both working full time and my attending law school several nights a week, we continued to date.

Ultimately, on November 6, 1999 in a horse-drawn carriage in the streets around the Faneuil Hall Marketplace of Boston, Massachusetts, she accepted my heart-felt proposal of marriage. Coincidentally, I would be sworn into the Massachusetts bar exactly three years later in that same Faneuil Hall.

We didn't have it all figured out back then. Heck, we don't have it all figured out now. But we entered into the lifelong marital relationship that has strengthened both of us and enabled us to share the joyful experiences that two imperfect people enjoy within the loving bonds of matrimony. Our marriage is a testament to my own experience and firm belief that we should not delay fully living our lives, even as we strive to grow in *The 10 Thriving Life Principles*.

Following our first few years of marriage and the purchase of our home, Kimberly and I were blessed to welcome Elizabeth Grace into our world one January evening, surrounded by family members. I recall that evening and the joy that Elizabeth has continued to bring to our family, even as I often sit in the very recliner that we purchased to provide Kimberly a comfortable place to relax during those midnight feedings.

Much as I continue to learn to be a better man through my marriage to Kimberly, so too has fatherhood helped me to grow in *The 10 Thriving Life Principles* as I've watched this amazing young lady grow from that vulnerable baby and inquisitive toddler into the accomplished Renaissance woman she is today.

Less Rules, Just Right

I have come to believe in a parenting variation on the old Outback Steakhouse slogan, which I refer to as "less rules, just right". One enduring experience from my own childhood was emblazoned in my memory—some rules that parents enforce on their children just don't make sense.

I could wax philosophical on the reasons why parents employ and enforce those rules, but simply I believe that parents either experienced these rules themselves, learned them from well-meaning people, or read about them in child-rearing books. Regardless, I determined that the rules I would employ should be grounded in common sense principles that I and our daughter could understand.

She lived through childhood and she is thriving today, so apparently we didn't screw things up, even if we did break with convention. So, what are some of the things we did or didn't do?

Bedtime

During her preschool years, Elizabeth always managed to let us know when she was tired each evening. We'd tuck her in and she'd wake up the next morning without any trouble. Even in those early years when our schedules meant that Kimberly was leaving the house in the pre-dawn hours to drop Elizabeth off at Aunt Rocky and Uncle Steve's house, Elizabeth thrived and quickly outgrew the need for naps.

As Kindergarten was approaching, Kimberly suggested that we should begin preparing Elizabeth to have a set bedtime that would allow her to adjust to a full-day school schedule. I had a different opinion, grounded in my own childhood memory of lying awake in bed many nights, often for an hour or more, because the bedtime didn't coincide with my natural energy level.

I suggested that we continue the variable schedule that had prevailed during the first five years. Kimberly agreed somewhat apprehensively. Elizabeth entered Kindergarten without the fixed bedtime constraint, continuing to let us know when she was ready to go to bed. And we never looked back.

Elizabeth progressed through elementary, middle, and into high school without issue. She generally went to bed between nine thirty and ten o'clock when she announced she was tired. Occasionally, she'd stay up until ten thirty or eleven to drain the last energy of the day. But she never had an issue rising at five thirty each morning to greet the following day.

She remained receptive to suggestions of going to sleep when an early rising or next day's events necessitated getting a little extra sleep. She excelled in academics, sports, and creative activities. All without a set bedtime. Even as a high school student, Elizabeth would often rise early during summer vacation to go out on a bike ride or work on a creative project, all without the aid of an alarm clock.

We kept the outcome in focus all those years, which was for Elizabeth to remain healthy and energetic to face whatever the following day required. She managed her mental and physical health, emotional attitude, and productive time effectively with our guidance, so as to honor the principles.

More importantly, Elizabeth developed her own self-discipline to manage her affairs well as a teen and young adult in an era when so many articles have decried the lack of responsibility exhibited by young people to transition to adulthood.

A Month Of Halloween Costumes

Halloween is its own funny little quirk in the lives of children. We spend a child's life warning them of stranger danger, avoiding unknown homes and vehicles, and not to accept anything from people we don't know.

Then one night a year, we turn those same children loose to walk up to dozens of strangers' homes and accept candy, even if there is an old creepy white van parked in the driveway down by the river. But often I have marveled at how parents prohibit their children from wearing the costume out beforehand (except to a party), so that it "doesn't get ruined". My opinion is, what the heck good is the costume after Halloween, so you may as well get the most use out of it as possible a-forehand.

Elizabeth developed a style of her own from an early age. One Halloween season during her preschool years she became enamored with dressing up in various made-up costumes and walking around the neighborhood to see houses decorated for the holiday.

But that one year, we were blessed with favorable weather in October. On many nights Elizabeth would walk with either Kimberly or me up and down different streets around the neighborhood to see the diversity of decorations. We weren't trick-or-treating any homes until the 31st, but in those fallen leaf days leading up to the big day, we laughed and we relished the lights and creatures we saw.

Living In A Zoo

My wife claims not to be a pet person, but she is a saint. She lives with two pet lovers, including me—a self-avowed pushover when it comes to allowing animals to live with us.

From the first guinea pig that she received from her cousin and the dozens of goldfish she won at the church festival during preschool, Elizabeth has loved her pets. Dozens more fish came and went, as did many rescued pets, including beloved guinea pigs, a gerbil, a cat, and a dog.

Elizabeth then intentionally bred hamsters (yes, with our knowledge). Our assent to this "experiment" had been inspired by her active involvement in 4-H and premised on her promise to secure homes in advance of breeding for the expected baby hamsters. Of the nine hamsters that were born of that litter, all adoption commitments fell through with the exception of one kind neighbor down the street. Including the four adult hamsters that we already owned, our family was left to care for twelve hamsters. Cleaning hamster cages became an assembly-line style chore that I do not seek to repeat any time soon. Although their lifespans are relatively short, the final member of that litter remained a vibrant member of our family for nearly 2 ½ years!

Bedtimes, Halloween costumes, and our Zoo are but a few of the memories that mark this great experiment in parenting that have allowed me to cherish our family even more across the years. We've transitioned into an era of electric guitars, skateboarding, and her desire for tattoos and piercings.

Admittedly, I don't have marriage or parenting all figured out, and that's part of what has made—and continues to make—this journey so much fun. I do know for sure that there aren't nearly as many hard and fast rules as some folks would lead you to believe.

We're all still cheating Death one day at a time. I'm still excited to grow in *Principle 6* daily. And I hope that you will be, too.

Taking Action: Cherishing Your Family To Win Your Amazing Life

As you have surmised, I love my family immensely. And there are so many additional extended family members and friends that I could share with you, but we'll save that for another time. Each of our families is unique, having its own dynamics, shared traditions, and diverse personalities.

Cherishing your family is a key to cheating Death and winning your amazing life. At each phase of your life, through the good times and the challenges, your family is the foundation and the pinnacle of all that you encounter together. No matter what form your family takes, from you and your parents to you and your grandchildren, and everything in between, your family is your family.

I encourage you to prioritize every minute of every day that you can around your family members, including your close friends. You can't predict how long you or those family members will remain together, so don't delay that kind word, that shared story, that meal, or that social event.

Career, chores, time, and money should never be used as excuses for failing to engage with those family members and close friends whom you cherish. True, we all have to earn a living and run errands to keep the home fires burning, but we mustn't get so bogged down in the minutiae that we miss out on those celebrations and reunions that so fuel our hearts and souls.

You might already be optimizing *Principle 6* in your own amazing life, and if you are, I applaud you. But if, like me, you think that you could spend some more time and energy growing in this area of your life, then I encourage you to start immediately.

We all have unique family situations and structures, but we

all share love in common with someone—or many someones. Take the time today to reflect on each of those special women and men, girls and boys. More than simply reflecting, make time to sit with them, call them, text them, video chat them, demonstrate your boundless love for them. As your heart overflows and you fall exhausted into bed at the end of the day, you will know that you were made to love and to be loved.

Cherish your family deeply and daily, and you will be well on your way to winning your own most amazing life.

◆ ◆ ◆

Living Your Own Amazing Life

Now it's your turn to pause and take action. Invest a few minutes to reflect upon these questions and when you are ready, write your responses in your *Cheating Death: The 10 Thriving Life Principles Journal* or in a notebook.

1. Take a few minutes to list the individual names of each of your cherished family members and close friends, and then look back over each name and think about at least one trait, memory, or story that makes you think about her or him.

2. Who are one or two family members or close friends that you will commit to investing more time and effort into strengthening your relationship? How would you like to begin this re-commitment to those key people in your life?

3. What other activities or time wasters have you been engaging in that have distracted you, consumed your time or impeded your effort to cherish your family as strongly as you could? What decisions or actions will you take today to delegate those activities or reduce those time wasters so that you can devote more time and effort to your loved ones?

PRINCIPLE 7: EXPAND YOUR COMMUNITY

"We have all known the long loneliness and we have learned that the only solution is love and that love comes with community."

~ DOROTHY DAY[13]

Our world here on Earth is the most populated and technologically advanced that it has ever been. Yet, many of the women and men I encounter are the loneliest that they have ever been. Why?

Rising standards of living and the ubiquitous internet have created a perception that we all are living better and more interconnected lives. Stories told and images splashed across the television, web, and social media sites often exemplify the aspirational and more favorable aspects of life, from perfect profile photos to exotic travel destinations, thereby reinforcing a perception that we should all be living amazingly abundant lives already.

Beneath the virtual veneer lies a timeless truth that real life is neither perfect nor exotic 24/7. While I am admittedly more familiar with the domestic experiences of the September 11,

2001 terrorist attacks, the financial crisis of 2007-2008, and natural disasters, I am well aware that global crises such as the COVID-19 virus, racial and ethnic injustice, and food insecurity impact us all regardless of geography.

At the risk of sounding apocalyptic, we will either come together as a global community comprised of interdependent cultures to solve the diverse challenges that we face, or we will eventually perish socially, politically, and financially as a species. Individually, that tension is what women and men struggle with daily as they seek to make an impact upon their local communities in every corner of the globe. But it doesn't have to be that way.

What Does It Mean To Expand Your Community?

As with each of *The 10 Thriving Life Principles*, *Principle 7* is intertwined with and dependent upon growth in each of its companion principles. In some ways, expanding your community is a logical extension of the progressive journey toward individual emotional mastery (*Principle 5: Embrace Emotional Bliss*) and collaborative family bonds (*Principle 6: Cherish Your Family*). Healthy communities are centered around love.

As we strengthen ourselves individually and as a family unit, we build upon that firm foundation to uplift our local and broader communities. But sometimes our efforts to strengthen our local communities provides the fuel that powers our individual and family progress. In other words, there is no single path to expanding your community. But failure to expand your community will hasten your isolation and societal obsolescence, denying you the opportunity to cheat Death.

Caring communities support stable families and strong nations. And caring communities depend upon individuals, businesses, and organizations to maintain and expand the positive impact that the community can exert. Therefore, the community is quite literally relying upon each of us to do our part.

When you love your community, you are lifting up not only the collective within your neighborhoods, but by extension you are lifting up and encouraging others to lift up the most vulnerable and marginalized among us.

Doing our part takes on as many unique characteristics as there are people in the community. From the child who participates in local youth sports or community recreation center arts & crafts activities, to the businesses that operate on Main Street, to the volunteers who ensure that senior citizens receive nutritious meals delivered to their homes, there are countless activities that comprise the lifeblood of our communities.

Sometimes women and men will question whether or not what they are doing (or propose to do) will have any impact upon the broader community. The answer is a resounding "YES"! There is no well-intentioned activity in which one could engage—individually or collectively—that will not contribute to the vitality of the community.

Like a painted masterpiece, while the individual brushstrokes may not all be cited publicly, the finished work of art will draw the attention of everyone for its beauty. Picking up trash in a public park may not seem like a big deal until everyone fails to pick up any trash, inviting overgrown weeds and senseless vandalism to subsume public spaces.

In the final analysis, any kind word that you can offer a neighbor, any act that you can do to improve the life of another, any product or service that you can offer to your local residents, will have the effect of expanding your community and inviting other women and men to also partake in the interactive life of your local and broader community.

You may be thinking that you're more of a private person, and not exactly the pillar of the community that you think you have to be. Fear not, because as you will see from my own journey, there is a place for each of us to expand our community.

How I Came To Expand My Community

I began my life as an introvert, one who draws energy from within. If my last *Meyers-Briggs Type Indicator*[14] personality profile was any indication, then that trait carried through into my adulthood. I had taken the personality test as a young adult in college, and then again a decade later after I had entered my career, and the results were remarkably similar.

Introversion does not imply that one is anti-social, but only that the individual draws energy from within. Whereas an extrovert has a tendency to draw energy from interactions with other individuals. But life is a social game. Playgrounds. Sports teams. School projects. All require interacting with others. So at some level, whether we have inclined toward introversion or extroversion, we all can find a way to speak up to involve ourselves in activities that involve other people. I, too, found my way slowly but surely.

Principle 7 didn't come naturally to me until well into adulthood. While seemingly second nature to me now, my ability to expand my community instead progressed as a gradual process as I grew to engage, elicit, and eventually empower others. Like each of the other principles, expanding my community has provided great joy and remains integral to cheating Death and living my most amazing life.

Engage

No matter where you are on the introversion/extroversion spectrum, engaging others is a step by step journey. Sure, if you're already an outgoing person, then meeting people and striking up a conversation may feel like second nature.

But if you're like many of us, engaging socially with others might present perceived obstacles of fear (of rejection, looking stupid, awkward conversations), or at least some hesitation. And that's ok. I've experienced all of those feelings and then some, and survived.

Engaging other people isn't a competition of how many "likes" you receive or how many "connections" you have, as on a social media platform. I came to understand that engaging other people is a matter of genuine quality. Better to meet one *quality* person each year than to race around a bar, a party, or a business conference meeting as many people as humanly possible, only to feel physically exhausted and emotionally devoid at the end of the night. I tried that and found that those make-busy activities often only left me more *disconnected* from my community.

Think about how you met your best friend, your spouse, or even a school or work friend. I bet you weren't even *trying* to meet that person. It just kind of happened, likely through an otherwise everyday conversation that carried over to the next time you ran into each other. Then the discussions took on more substance as you both began to elicit details about something you had in common.

Whether meeting people just comes naturally, or you need to consciously pay attention to it, the end game isn't simply to *meet* that person, but to get to *know them* and to let them get to know *you*. I have come to really enjoy meeting new people and getting to know them in a personal way. Truly engaging with people will come to feel natural and pleasant.

Elicit

Getting to know people is kind of like trying that new restaurant that opened up in your neighborhood. You're bound to find something you like, but you may have to try several items until you truly find that special dish that excites your palette.

You may have found a new person yourself, or someone introduced you to a new person. But either way, you end up talking to
this new person. You can only spend so much time talking about
the weather before that gets dull and runs out of steam. Therefore, you've got to pivot to talking about something of more
substance if you're planning to keep the conversation going.

Depending upon the circumstances under which we met, I
have found that the path of our discussion can go in many
different directions. But the common theme is that I genuinely want to elicit information about the other person that
helps me to weigh how much we two might have in common. You're not going to click with every woman or man you
encounter.

If you're at a youth sporting event watching your child play
a game, then asking questions about the other person's child is
natural. Trying the same thing under different circumstances
might appear awkward or creepily personal. Eliciting information in a discussion also isn't a competition or a race. It should
be relaxed, natural, and mutually fun.

I start with topics of assumed commonality. Often times the
circumstances or surroundings will help this to happen naturally. At a training class or a business conference, I can assume
that the women and men that I encounter have some common
career interests, experiences, or goals. I suggest starting there,
asking a question as simple as "how did you get interested in becoming X?"

You can stay on a topic for as long as the other individual is
comfortable talking about it. I can't tell you how many times
that I've shared an entire meal with someone, and never got off
of a subject because my new companion was so excited to talk
about it. Absolutely nothing wrong with that, especially if the
other person is happy and energized discussing that topic. Be-

coming a better listener is still something I'm working on, but listening to others is always a surefire way to enjoy meeting new people.

Most conversations develop into back-and-forth exchanges, but I am a big believer that we should let the other person talk for as long as practical. When that individual leaves you, she/he will know that they have been heard and appreciated. In addition to elevating their own self-esteem, that person will be more inclined to speak well of you to others and to seek out your companionship the next time you run into each other.

Don't worry about trying to fit too much into the initial conversation, because if the exchange is destined to develop into a longer-term relationship, you will have ample opportunities to speak about yourself in the future. And yet some of the greatest interactions are the ones that stand alone, and due to circumstances, never actually recur. There's absolutely no wasted interpersonal engagement if you feel that you've connected with another individual in a positive manner. Sometimes you just weren't destined to ever see that person again, and that's ok.

Building a community moves well beyond initially engaging in activities and developing relationships with other women and men. In addition to engaging with others in fulfilling discussions by eliciting information in a mutual exchange, you also will often find yourself in a position to empower the other individual. Communities are strengthened through empowerment, where everyone wins.

Empower

Living my life fully has freed me from doubts and concerns that may previously have held me back. With that freedom and my enjoyment of engaging others in social conversations, I found myself increasingly in situations where other people were looking to me for validation, support, or even expert guidance. Initially, this newfound attraction caught me by surprise, but it will happen to you, too.

While this role is not one that should inflate your own ego, it is a role that you should take very seriously. The credibility with which you carry yourself is attractive to others, because they know that you have genuinely put these principles into action in your own life. They see you succeeding at living your best life. They develop trust in you.

Your genuine social interactions demonstrate your willingness to engage non-judgmentally with women and men from all walks of life. You are telegraphing that you have either walked a mile in their shoes or you know someone who did. Others are attracted to your humility, your patience, and your candor.

Understand the power that your winning attitude and positive encouragement can have on others. Your own family and friends will feel it. Your co-workers and employees will feel it. The people you encounter at restaurants, stores, and social events will feel it.

Your social engagement takes on an entirely new dimension in addition to simply enjoying a nice chat over a cup of coffee. You will be making a difference in people's lives, giving them the additional energy to take risks, make incremental progress on personal or professional goals, and celebrate even the small successes en route to cheating Death and more fully living their own best lives.

Taking Action: Expand Your Community To Win Your Amazing Life

We are created as social beings. You may already have mastered *Principle 7* in your own amazing life prior to even picking up this book. If so, I applaud you and encourage you to continue to help others of us to do the same.

But if you're like many of us who are still traveling the journey of *The 10 Thriving Life Principles*, then you know that expanding your community is likely a work in progress that never truly ends. We can all begin somewhere, and we should begin today, even if with but one small step.

No matter how much our technology and employment trends have allowed us to telecommute via Zoom meetings and office from coffee shops, we crave and thrive on the social interaction inherent to our nature as human beings.

While social media allows us a certain degree of human interaction, it cannot and does not replace the in-person connection that energizes our spirits and creativity. Face-to-face interactions that allow us to receive and respond to social cues are lost in the two-dimensional digital exchange of texts, DMing, and email. At least you can "hear" someone smiling during a telephone conversation.

So where do we begin to rebuild that social framework in our lives? Begin by engaging other people in a more direct manner. Elicit as much information as you comfortably can and share as much about yourself as you wish. Don't concern yourself with empowering others right off the bat, but certainly remain aware of opportunities where you may do so.

You can expand your community simply by saying hello to your neighbors or the women and men you encounter as you go about your daily errands. Ask the clerk at the checkout counter how she or he is doing today, and then actively listen to their response. Attend your child's sporting events with more regularity and offer to volunteer your assistance to the coach or the concession stand. Attend a parade, a local community theatre, or a craft fair to support local performers and artisans. And the list goes on and on.

There is no wrong way to expand your community. Simply get outside of your home. Share smiles and kind words with people whom you encounter, pausing long enough to honestly listen to what they say in reply. Learn to say "YES" when asked to volunteer or participate in a community activity.

Trust your instincts about the activities you wish to engage in and the places you wish to go. And as you go about your day, consciously lift up others as they engage in their activities. Recognize leadership potential and proactivity in younger people and those who may come from disadvantaged circumstances.

Together, we are stronger. Together, we *are* the Community.

Living Your Own Amazing Life

Now it's your turn to pause and take action. Invest a few minutes to reflect upon these questions and when you are ready, write your responses in your *Cheating Death: The 10 Thriving Life Principles Journal* or in a notebook.

1. What are some of the reasons that you may have hesitated in the past to get more involved in your community?

2. Describe one of two local activities or places that you would like to learn more about?

3. What skills, experiences, or knowledge do you possess that could be of benefit to younger members of your community if you shared them?

PRINCIPLE 8: EXTEND OPPORTUNITY EQUITABLY

"We all should know that diversity makes for a rich tapestry, and we must understand that all the threads of the tapestry are equal in value no matter what their color."

~ MAYA ANGELOU[15]

In My DNA

My paternal grandfather was an art director with an advertising house in Manhattan, and had met my grandmother while they attended Pratt Institute in the late 1930s. Both from New England, they found New York City to be intellectually rich, socially vibrant and conducive to making a living. After they married, my grandparents settled down in a tiny Brooklyn walkup flat at a time when they could walk for blocks without seeing an automobile parked on the streets on their way to the Brooklyn Bridge.

My father was born and raised in Brooklyn, and had met my mother when he attended William Cullen Bryant High School in Astoria, Queens in the mid-1960s. I wouldn't realize until many years later that my mother hadn't attended her 1967 senior prom with my father, but instead with an African-American friend named Douglas. After my parents split up, I recall my mother continuing to date without racial distinctions well into my own adulthood.

After living in my maternal grandparents' home until I was six months old, I moved with my mother and father to a variety of walkup flats in Staten Island and Brooklyn, eventually settling in on the ninth floor of a building at Willoughby Walk beside my paternal grandparents' building.

I didn't know that I was different until that second year of pre-school, when the *second* little white kid showed up at my nursery school. Heck, I don't remember his name, but his pasty white freckled skin offset by his red hair remains unmistakably in my memory.

I think he thought that he had a natural kinship to me as he tried to befriend me, but all I saw was that he was taking the attention away from me! When I had arrived at Herman Hannahan Nursery School in that nondescript Brooklyn brownstone in the early 1970s, I enjoyed the attention focused on *me*. Kids marveled at my towhead pin-straight blonde hair and pale skin. I learned (and long ago since forgot) how to count to ten in Swahili and other words and phrases.

It may sound cliché, but I hadn't really noticed that all of my schoolmates and teachers were African-American, or that my bland clothing contrasted with their array of brightly colored cultural prints that marked the era. After all, I lived on the edge of Bed-Stuy, so my daily life blended race, ethnicity, and culture as easily as the produce section at the little A&P on Myrtle Avenue blended the rainbow of fruits and vegetables. My mother's second husband, my stepfather, was a man of color. Further, my grandparents had long maintained a diverse circle of friends since before my father was born, such that race, ethnicity, gender, and sexual preference were liberally interwoven into our lives and literally omnipresent in our apartments.

My early childhood multicultural palette was reduced to a can of flat white paint when I moved to Rhode Island to live with my father and begin first grade. While traces of immigrant Anglo-European ethnic diversity abounded across the state, *racial diversity* was invisible to me in our working-class Warwick and West Warwick neighborhoods. And even more so when we moved to West Greenwich for fifth grade.

What Does It Mean To Extend Opportunity Equitably?

> *"...THAT guy is talking to US about diversity, equity and inclusion?!..."*

Oh, yes, I have heard the occasional whisper and the even more rare loud-enough-meant-for-me-to-hear retort over the decades. In the early days, I winced a bit, but in later years I've simply smiled.

Many horrible events dating back to before the founding of our nation and continuing to this day underscore the inequity that has plagued all facets of our society. No single one of us, woman or man, black or white, Muslim or Christian, can erase the emotional pain, financial oppression, and physical death that has been visited upon the many by the sadistic minority of citizens that spew racial, ethnic, and cultural hatred.

Silence is violence. But banded together in a mutual commitment to all that is good and possible for our human race, can we strive hour by hour, day by day to extend opportunity equitably to every individual based solely upon her or his merit. Together, we can cheat Death by overwhelming it with our collective action. When we extend opportunity equitably, we are simply loving each individual for whom she or he is as a fellow human being.

Embracing diversity

Diversity is not a political position for me. It is simply a matter of ethical principle. In fact, in a meritocracy whose foundation is equitable access for all who actively seek opportunity, I cannot imagine why anyone would oppose diversity.

I do strongly believe in valuing diversity, and do not subscribe to the notion that individuals should downplay or assimilate those self-ascribed cultural, ethnic, racial, and familial internal and external traits that mark their own uniqueness. We consciously choose not to place limitations on others who themselves may have rejected the notion that they have any limitations, physical, emotional, or otherwise. We must celebrate all that we are and those who have come before us to make us who we are.

When each of us are able to bring our full selves into every situation—vocationally, educationally, socially—then we are able to compete equitably for each opportunity in which we demonstrate an interest. As a leader, I have always sought to have the best ideas brought to every discussion, and I contend that women and men will only bring forth those best ideas when they are confident that they are operating in a welcoming environment.

Thus, while traits and characteristics do not of themselves ascribe a preference to one individual over another for the receipt of an unearned benefit, an attitude that wholly embraces diversity will remove false impediments from consideration in each interaction. Once each woman and man is unchained from the false constructs of historical racism, sexism, xenophobia, and other ignorant and baseless constraints, then she and he may embrace each opportunity and compete based on her or his own merits.

Embracing diversity allows leaders and teams to establish free and fair atmospheres in which everyone learns, works, and plays at their best. Victories are earned solely on each individual having demonstrated her or his mastery of the particular objective.

My orientation toward embracing diversity has allowed me to meet, befriend, and collaborate with some of the most amazing people in a multitude of educational, community, and professional arenas. That being said, I don't pretend to fully understand each person's troubled walk through discriminatory circumstances, nor can I expect every individual to reconcile my today with my Brooklyn beginning and challenging past.

I did not grow up with privilege, white or otherwise. Like many of you, I worked diligently to overcome my socioeconomic disadvantages and often did not prevail when others were more qualified than me. Whatever I have achieved, I have done so meritoriously, and feel neither guilt nor the need to apologize for earning my place in this diverse world.

The Great Equalizer

For me, I will not be satisfied simply that every individual is granted entrance into the dance hall, nor will I be satisfied merely to ensure that every individual gets invited to dance...but that EVERY individual could have the opportunity to LEAD the dance if she or he is willing to put forth the effort to do so. You know what I mean.

Despite my upbringing, I do not consider myself to be politically liberal. In fact, I would characterize myself as more of a fiscal conservative since my youth. But implicit in being fiscally conservative is my belief that *only* those facts that matter should matter when it comes to accessing opportunity. If, based on the objective facts, you are the best qualified woman or man to earn an award, a scholarship, a promotion, etc., then you should receive that which you have earned.

Education is the great equalizer. Access to education, to community activities, to social engagements, and so forth should be afforded to *every* girl and boy, to *every* woman and man, regardless of immutable characteristics. But once the access has been granted, let us not fool ourselves into believing that every person *afforded* the access will put forth equivalent *effort* to achieve the potential outcomes.

When I was standing up one of the nation's first corporate diversity programs in the 1990s at one of the largest financial institutions in the United States, I emphasized that providing equal access to opportunity was table stakes. If we didn't provide the equal access, then how could we be certain that we would be attracting the highest quality pool of potential candidates for each role. We worked diligently to build trust among employees that they would truly be valued for their skills, experiences, and abilities, and the results years later proved the effectiveness of our approach.

Children cannot dictate the circumstances into which they are born, and have limited control over the circumstances in which they are raised. But from the moment opportunities are provided by family members, neighbors, teachers, coaches, and local business people, it becomes incumbent upon that child to begin seeking, competing for, and optimizing each appropriate opportunity that is presented.

Even in the most financially-strapped public schools, caring teachers and staff may be found. Countless stories abound of children who have capitalized on slim academic, athletic, and extra-curricular opportunities to claw their way out of the bleakness. While many children of all races and ethnicities may lack both the inner drive and the adult support at home, there are enough examples of women and men who made the most out of limited opportunities to rise up to great heights of power and prestige in their adulthood.

Persons of color have been elected President and Vice President of the United States and Senators, confirmed as Supreme Court Justices, Secretary of Defense, and Secretary of State, selected as the Chair of the Joint Chiefs of Staff of the Military, hired as corporate CEOs, and so forth. Not once have I heard any of those women and men attribute their position to racially- or gender-based hiring preferences. Excellence reflects and celebrates diversity.

No Excuses

I do believe that each person should have the *access* to compete to *achieve* those outcomes. I do not believe that we are all *entitled* to equal *outcomes*, because I don't believe that everyone of any race or ethnicity is willing to work as hard as her or his peer to achieve those outcomes. I don't believe in excuses, but I do belief in effort.

Yet, even today, we see individuals of every socioeconomic, gender, racial, ethnic, and cultural background simply ignore the opportunities that are being presented to them. Whether the child of a millionaire or a millwright, a girl or boy who squanders the available academic, athletic, and extracurricular opportunities to instead engage in wasteful, unhealthy, or unproductive activities has *chosen* to forego achievement.

We do not need to make allowances and excuses to elevate laggards into a consolation round with true achievers. When I failed to take full advantage of opportunities in my life, that was on me—not my race, not my "upbringing", not my "environment". Certainly, we all can re-enter ourselves into the fray time and time again, but we should be prepared to get serious about putting forth the effort and competing to achieve the outcomes that others have already demonstrated that they were willing to compete for.

How I Came To Extend Opportunity Equitably

I really didn't find myself returning to a racially diverse neigh-borhood until I moved to Houston in the mid-1980s. Racial and ethnic diversity abounded, including my first real introduction to a significant Vietnamese-American population that had re-settled to the Texas Gulf Coast from their traumatic 1975 war-time exodus.

While I had heard racial slurs during my lifetime in New Eng-land, I was shocked at the ease and frequency with which slurs were slung around in Houston by my new white teen associates at my large high school in the Aldine Independent School Dis-trict on the fringe of the Houston city limits.

While racial diversity was well-represented visually, the socioeconomic undercurrent markedly divided African-Ameri-can, Hispanic, Asian, and White students. Simultaneously serv-ing an upper-crust golf course community, sprawling working class apartment complexes, and a well-entrenched ghetto, the school represented a universe of cultural planets that orbited but did not touch, except when they occasionally collided. With underemployment suppressing our daily existence at home in our apartment following my mother's foreclosure, I was surprised to learn later on that my newfound friends had wrongly assumed that we "had money".

Because my own dating patterns broadly mirrored that of my mother's own youth, I had to contend with both the direct verbal attacks of strangers in public, as well as my own friends' raised eyebrows and thinly-veiled questions. I was uncomfort-able with the overt racism and ethnic slurs, and occasionally created my own stumbles by overcorrecting in the opposite direction. During my first term at my new high school, I pre-sented a history paper on the Ku Klux Klan that included scathing modern-day references to its presence and alleged prevalence in Texas. That well-researched paper won me nothing but the scorn of my classmates directed toward a carpetbagger come lately.

I have never suffered from guilt over supposed white privilege, and when I enrolled at Texas A&M University, I continued to seek to broaden my understanding of the diverse racial and ethnic cultures of which I was a part. Making friends was easy at the dormitory, in my classes, and within various student organizations. My multiracial, multicultural dating activity continued to enrich my social tapestry at college, much as it had in high school, and I seemed to receive fewer direct insults.

Academically, I was surprised to find that I was one of only a handful of white students who enrolled that semester in an African-American American History elective. I was even more taken aback at how I was viewed skeptically by several of my fellow students as if I had an "agenda" for even being there. Sometimes it helps my own understanding to be on the receiving end of that rude behavior which another has experienced for her or his entire life.

When I rushed Greek letter organizations my second year at college, I was invited to consider multiple fraternities. But when I also approached a friend of mine about whether I would be considered eligible for his chapter, M.A. politely explained to me that Alpha Phi Alpha probably "wasn't quite ready" for me and encouraged me to continue rushing the other fraternities that I had been invited to consider. Drawn by the friendships and all that its standards represent, I was honored to ultimately pledge and become a Life Loyal Member of the Sigma Chi Fraternity.

My inner attraction to promoting equitable and inclusive opportunity didn't end in my youth, and would continue strongly as I continued into my post-graduate and professional journey as an ally and advocate for others.

Open Doors And Break Glass Ceilings

"Cris, thanks for the boost to finally ask my SVP
for that grad school recommendation! I knew
she's an alum, but your post gave me the belief
that she would actually WANT to help me..."

Indeed, my friend. Indeed!

Asking often delivers the YES that opens doors. Never fail to ask.

When asked, find a way to say YES. Remember that someone said YES to YOU many years ago.

Three leaders I knew willingly wrote my law school recommendations:

• a U.S. Senator (former Secretary of the Navy & State Governor)
• a wheelchair-bound U.S. Congressman
• an esteemed National Bank President

...The one guy who refused? Mid-level white corporate executive who felt that my unconventional journey "didn't deserve his recommendation." Ok, Boomer!

"Cris, you're my white guy ally!"

I chuckled when I heard it put that way, but it's an accurate variation of labels applied to me for my nearly 30 years in the Diversity, Equity, and Inclusion (DEI) space (back to when it was all neatly termed "diversity").

Thanks to all who courageously ask me to share their journey, online and offline. I learn and grow each day, and you know that I've always got your back.

*"Cris, I love partnering with you to speak to folks
about equity and inclusion. But even more, I
appreciate that you actually open doors for us."*

People know that I'm not often without words...but my long-time colleague's remark reminded me that mere words--without concrete daily actions--would simply be feel-good political correctness. We've got too much of that already! While sense-less deaths of innocent people of color at the hands of racists have dominated the news and woken the national conscience in a profound manner, I have been woke for decades.

Champions and mentors opened doors for me. It's my commit-ment to emerging leaders to always extend that same commit-ment. I have lived my professional life as an expression of that genuine love for my team members and colleagues, opening doors and breaking through glass ceilings with them, resulting in many women and men having risen to significance through their own merit. Thank you for inviting me to share your jour-ney.

Taking Action: Extending Opportunity Equitably To Win Your Amazing Life

You're not THAT important. Think on that truth before you withhold your support. Given our own success, you and I have been entrusted with a stewardship to open doors. We may be female or male, black or white, foreign- or native-born, and so forth. It doesn't matter—open doors and break glass ceilings for other people.

I'm not suggesting that you interview, hire, promote, or advo-cate on behalf of any individual who is not qualified for a role. It doesn't matter whether we're talking about an academic op-portunity, a youth sports team, a community leadership post, etc.—choose the best qualified candidate(s). But *do not fail* to provide access to any qualified individual to compete for the role(s).

Don't prejudge based on immutable characteristics, background, prior shortcomings, and the like. People will surprise you by how well they can outperform your own limiting beliefs. Underdogs and second-chance competitors will often invest so much more into an opportunity than you yourself might have been willing to invest. Don't close the door of opportunity on anyone until they have either failed to step through the door, or they have failed to achieve the minimum standard to compete.

Will you exercise your power to promote others, or will you preserve society's perceived prerogative for those people they deem more worthy? Servant leaders like you and I are endowed by our Creator to embrace the stewardship to uplift this next generation of emerging leaders. Give of yourself generously and often.

Stay humble. You and I owe it to our next generation of emerging leaders to open that door. This willingness to support and advocate for others as they launch themselves into new phases of their lives has paid daily dividends in my own life. I smile each time I receive a DM, text, or call from another woman or man who has secured an internship, a fellowship, or a promotion, because she or he confidently approached a leader with a request that was very willingly granted.

Thank you for sharing your DEI journey with me, and helping me to widen the dance floor. Together, we've got this!

Living Your Own Amazing Life

Now it's your turn to pause and take action. Invest a few minutes to reflect upon these questions and when you are ready, write your responses in your *Cheating Death: The 10 Thriving Life Principles Journal* or in a notebook.

1. Describe a time in your own life where someone prejudged your ability to participate in or compete for an opportunity. How did that exclusion make you feel?

2. What has been your own track record with providing equal access to opportunity to others in your own community or profession?

3. Describe one or two ways that you can more effectively leverage your own community visibility or professional authority to ally with and advocate on behalf of girls and boys, women and men from historically-underrepresented groups?

PRINCIPLE 9: ACHIEVE FINANCIAL SECURITY

"Money will not purchase happiness for the man who has no concept of what he wants: money will not give him a code of values, if he's evaded the knowledge of what to value, and it will not provide him with a purpose, if he's evaded the choice of what to seek. Money will not buy intelligence for the fool, or admiration for the coward, or respect for the incompetent."

~ FRANCISCO D'ANCONIA[16]

I would suggest that you can be well on your way to living an amazing life without having yet mastered *Principle 9*. Thus, achieving financial security is very deliberately reserved for *Principle 9*, as opposed to being addressed earlier in our discussion together.

As I mentioned at the outset of *Cheating Death: The 10 Thriving Life Principles*, this is not a book about getting rich quick. While I do not underestimate the positive impact that achieving financial security has had upon the lives of those women and men who do so, I also am careful not to over prioritize the focus on finances to the detriment of the first eight principles.

Financial Insecurity

I am accountable. I caused the financial calamities in my youth that required me to spend much of my younger adulthood making amends. Having grown up without role models of financial security, I failed to learn an approach to *Principle 9* until I had so thoroughly violated the principle as to be on the brink of bankruptcy. My life then became a journey back from the brink to eventually achieve the financial security that had always been available to me, but for my own missteps.

I had grown up in an environment where finances were rarely discussed around me as a child. When the subject of money did arise, it was framed in stark terms of scarcity and fear that drove inconsistent decision-making that further led to unnecessarily dire results in my childhood home. Financial insecurity became a whirlpool that swallowed emotional stability, relationships, and quality family time.

From an early age, I thus learned that my own financial future would be dependent upon my own efforts. And while I understood how to translate my work ethic into financial reward, my failure to understand the self-discipline necessary to effectively plan, save, and leverage my income led to my own youthful whirlpool. Having come from a scarcity mindset in my childhood home, I proceeded to spend every last dollar that I earned or received.

As a child, I spent my money on thousands of baseball cards, toys, music and video arcades. As a teenager, I got my first credit card at the age of seventeen. I filled a closet with name-brand clothing that I couldn't truly afford to impress people who really didn't notice or care what I wore. In college, I kept applying for credit to fuel an endless social life of restaurants, night clubs, and other boondoggles. I was fighting with collection agencies while my peers were earning their degree. Before I ever earned my college degree, I had my car repossessed for which I would continue to pay down that deficiency balance for a couple more years.

Thus, in my early twenties, I was a young adult riding a bicycle to work in the rain, to a job where I earned meager wages, and could barely put food in my apartment refrigerator. Rock bottom found me living out of my car, trekking across country so that I could beg my way back into living temporarily in my childhood home. Forcibly humbled, I found myself facing *Principle 1*, having to come to terms with the financial mess that I had caused and determining how I would recover and never repeat the mistakes.

Not only had I *not* achieved financial security, but I had so perverted the concept of what money meant in my young life, that I had ruined my credit and subverted my own intellectual, emotional, and vocational journey. I was a broke college dropout living back at home who had strayed so far off the path that it would literally take a decade before I would regain my financial footing and enjoy a renewed embrace of *Principle 9*.

What Does It Mean To Achieve Financial Security?

Financial security is achieved as the result of engendering financial literacy, employing a solid work ethic, and exercising self-discipline. Financial literacy has been defined by many different organizations, but it is essentially the education and understanding of knowing how money is made, spent, and saved, as well as the skills and ability to use financial resources to make well-planned decisions. These decisions include how to generate, invest, spend, and save money.

A work ethic may be thought of as the principle that hard

work is intrinsically virtuous or worthy of rewards, financial or otherwise. Self-discipline is the ability you have to control and motivate yourself, to remain focused on your objectives, and to avoid distractions and detractors from those objectives. Without a work ethic or self-discipline, you not only will fail to cheat Death, but will instead actually hasten Death's inevitable visit. We recommit our love for ourselves and those who depend upon us for support by exercising our self-discipline and work ethic to honor our financial commitments and build a better tomorrow.

Achieving financial security reveals itself to each woman and man what she or he envisions that it will be. There is no ultimate financial figure that defines what financial security means universally. *Principle 9* flows forth from and works interdependently with the realization of the first eight principles. The achievement of financial security pays its dividends in peace of mind, free from the distraction of needless worry.

Achieving financial security is grounded in the wisdom of the ages. Those who focus upon obtaining money and other property to the exclusion of the first eight principles are likely to neither achieve financial security nor enjoy the amazing life that is abundantly available to them. Similarly, those who are miserly with the money they do obtain will often find themselves plagued with unnecessary angst over the potential loss of their supposed wealth. As my own missteps have demonstrated on my journey to live this most amazing life, undue focus on money through overwork and miserliness can wreak havoc well beyond financial insecurity.

There is no single method to achieving financial security nor is there a cut-off time beyond which an individual would be prevented from its realization. Common threads of achieving financial security include focusing one's attention on achieving specific goals, exercising self-discipline for extended periods of time, and engaging in informed risk-taking. None of these threads are attached to predefined levels of measurement of total accumulation nor generally bounded by income level. We are all familiar with the accounts of women and men who toiled their entire lives earning a modest income into retirement, and then subsequently bequeathed staggering sums to noble causes upon their death.

Financial security may often be more readily achieved when you are passionately pursuing your life's mission without focusing unduly upon compensation. A belief in the boundless abundance of financial security arms successful leaders in all walks of life to bring others along on the journey to enjoy and master *Principle 9*. From entrepreneurs and business executives to teachers and parents, the lessons of *Principle 9* are best understood when they are shared in the active living of the preceding eight principles.

I have experienced this in my own life. The bottom line is that when you believe there is enough financial abundance for everyone to enjoy, then you will unleash yourself to plan, earn, leverage, and achieve financial security to support your most amazing life.

How I Came To Achieve Financial Security

You will recall that financial security is achieved as the result of engendering financial literacy, employing a solid work ethic, and exercising self-discipline. While I lacked the first and third elements as I careened into young adulthood, I had perfected my work ethic at a very young age as a survival mechanism. My work ethic hadn't been able to compensate for the twin holes of financial illiteracy and deficient self-discipline as I outspent my earnings. But when I did eventually hit rock bottom, I was able to rebuild upon the firm foundation of my work ethic.

As trite as it sounds, when I found myself at my lowest financial point, there was no place but up for me to go. I practiced *Principle 1* by necessity, and the inventory was pretty bleak. But despite advice from others that I should have considered filing for bankruptcy, my ethical standards would not allow me to walk away from the agreements that I had made. No matter how stupid my credit card overspending had been or how daunting the repossessed vehicle deficiency balance appeared, I knew that I had contracted for the benefit of my bargains. I, thus, remained accountable for my actions.

A word about blaming others for our financial mistakes. No one held a gun to my head and forcibly made me apply for the credit cards, obtain the vehicle loan, or incur the student loans. I am disgusted by the trend in our society to blame lenders or educational institutions for student loan debt, when the debt itself was a mutual contract that each student entered into *voluntarily* to obtain and repay funds. The loan was never intended to be a promise to secure employment as a result of the education.

Education plus hard work and building relationships, regardless of whether funded by student loans or not, is the key to obtaining career success. If you don't want to repay student loans, then postpone entering college until you have saved the money to attend. The only student loan "forgiveness" I sought was to honor the commitment that I made and repay every last dollar that I had received. To do otherwise would have been unethical.

Recognizing that my debt reduction outlay required me to reduce my discretionary expenses to near zero, I focused my attention on the income lever. In my early twenties, I turned to what I knew would be the fastest way for me to generate cash flow, capitalizing on my prior experience in the hospitality industry.

The restaurant business was the intersection of several paths on my life journey. I knew from an early age that it was also a gateway to a successful life for me that would extend far beyond the casual theme dining locales that I favored. It was there that I transformed myself from a shy kid afraid of public speaking into an engaging salesperson who mastered the secrets to selling the sizzle that led to my great success as a banker and an attorney many years later.

Pecan Pie And Sweet Tea

My introduction to the restaurant business was through the common fast food route. When I turned sixteen, I had gotten my first official job at a chain called Grandy's, whose southern fare included smoked ribs, freshly battered fried chicken, and oven-baked rolls. As a transplanted northerner, I was also introduced to the notion that there were two kinds of iced tea, and folks were very particular about which kind (unsweetened or pre-sweetened with sugar) they drank.

Lucky for me, the restaurant was located within walking distance from our apartment. I was hired in as a cashier, and quickly came to realize that I was expected to up sell each order that I took.

One of the big draws to Grandy's were our sweet rolls, and we sold them by the dozen as often as we sold them individually. People would come through the drive through just to take home the sweet rolls. But sometimes we would focus on other menu items.

One night I happened to be working the drive through, when our manager challenged us to a pecan pie selling contest I was enthusiastic about participating in a contest, and began offering the deliciously sticky pie to each customer as they placed their order over the speaker.

I didn't comprehend why several customers didn't seem to understand what I was offering them. Then my manager came over and gently let me know that I wasn't saying it right. Huh?

Well, because I was newly transplanted from the northeastern part of the United States, I was offering the customers what I had grown up calling '*pee*-can' pie. The manager explained to me that in Texas and throughout the south it was (*correctly*) called 'pe-*con*' pie. While it took me a little while to remember to consistently place the emphasis on the word in the local fashion, my sales did immediately take off.

The pecan pie lesson and other lessons that I would learn from my managers and co-workers would pay off during my tenure at Grandy's. Previously a shy, self-conscious kid, I grew to love interacting with our customers. Leveraging the work ethic that had garnered me odd jobs throughout my childhood, I learned to set up, close down, and deep clean a restaurant efficiently with my co-workers.

As time went on, I took on more responsibility, becoming known as the go-to kid. I'd pick up the extra Friday night shift that a fellow teen parted with to go to a party. I'd come in on last-minute notice to take a shift for a no-show co-worker on a Sunday morning. I even became our back-up cook one day when the cook quit on a busy shift, leaving me to apply common sense to the guidance that my harried manager was giving me through the pass-through window as he waited on customers. I learned to batter and deep-fry fresh chicken that day, and earned additional respect from my leaders.

I ended up winning company-sponsored sales and service competitions, and eventually took on a role as a shift leader. I was putting in a full-time schedule while managing my high school education, and learning to live on less sleep than many of my classmates. But I was developing my mantra that no one was going to be able to outwork me.

Beside the lessons learned about delivering world-class sales and service, versatility, and leadership, there was also a very practical motive to my employment. I worked as many closing shifts as possible, even switching off with closers to allow them to go home. You see, when I closed, I got to take home unsold food.

In the economic situation that we found ourselves at home, bringing home food that would otherwise have gone into the dumpster at the end of the night—fried chicken, baked rolls, or cinnamon rolls—was a dividend above and beyond my paycheck. This "food dividend" would be a hallmark of my job choices for many years to come, one for which I look back fondly with gratitude.

The Kettle

After high school, I went away to college at Texas A&M University in College Station. Despite my college scholarships and stipends that I had earned, I had allowed my poor money management skills to lead me to seek employment to maintain my chaotic social life. I happened to be studying at a diner that I and many others students frequented at night, when I got the idea that earning tips at this busy restaurant might be my ticket to remaining afloat financially. After all, I attended classes all day, but The Kettle was open 24 hours, so I figured that I could work there at night.

I spoke to my waitress, filled out and application that night, and came in for the interview the next day. I could sense immediately that the manager wasn't that excited to interview me. As I looked at the morning staff, it became more apparent that his entire waitstaff were women. He confirmed as much that they'd never hired a guy to wait tables, and he was concerned that I wouldn't last long because I was a college student.

I wasn't trying to make a gender-barrier breaking statement with my application, but I needed the money. And I knew from my prior work experiences that I could do this job, and said as much. It was at this moment that providence came to my rescue in the persona of the head waitress, Cheryl. She knew me from my frequency in the restaurant, so she spoke up to the manager and vouched for me, reassuring him that she would personally train me and be responsible for me.

Skeptical though he was, the manager trusted his long-time employee, and I was conditionally granted the job. Though I would train with Cheryl on the day shift due to her seniority, once trained I would be relegated to the less desirable overnight shift.

Because I had managed working full time in high school, I was confident that I'd be able to manage coming home at dawn to prepare for my classes. Reality would prove to be much harsher, as my plummeting academic grades would eventually bear out.

As my experience would confirm over many years, most people don't choose a long-term non-management career in the restaurant business. It just kind of happens that a short-term need turns into decades. Cheryl wasn't one to divulge long philosophical histories of her own life path that led her to remain at The Kettle so long, but she was a superb waitress and was willing to teach me everything she knew. Cheryl's lessons would help me as I transitioned to my professional career in public accounting.

Sell An Exceptional Product

"Cris, I can't hire you...you don't have ANY public accounting experience."

"Well, Mr. Sanders, that second part is true, so why don't you try me out for free for a week?..."

Real pitch from my own life. Sometimes you have to stick your foot in the door to keep it from closing prematurely.

Mr. Sanders didn't take me up on the no-pay offer, but he and his partner Mr. West DID hire me that day.

The lesson here? Stop making excuses. Simply be exceptional and ask for the opportunity to demonstrate your own capability.

You are your own amazing product. Be so confident in your competence that you could afford to give a prospective buyer a free trial. If you are the best option, then no other immutable characteristics matter in my book.

Of course, you must put the preparation in place beforehand and outwork your potential competitors before making such a claim. But if YOU don't have the confidence to sell your superiority above the competition, then why should anyone else hire you? You are the product of your superior skills and work ethic, so why wouldn't you sell yourself to achieve ultimate professional and financial success?

So, when I had to rebuild myself financially on the merits of my work ethic, I turned to the one person on whom I could always bet on and win—ME!

Relying upon the kindness of friends who could vouch for me, I initially tackled my debts digging ditches at a state prison complex for a commercial heating and cooling contractor, and providing labor on a commercial landscaping crew. I returned to the hospitality industry with two full-time jobs waiting tables, before I began the pivot toward my professional life.

I had strengthened my financial literacy through reading and leveraging the practical advice of those who had gone before me. Capitalizing on college jobs that I had held in public accounting, corporate finance, and banking, I returned to the banking industry as a contract employee. My willingness to perform whatever tasks were asked of me in combination with my ability to quickly synthesize disparate information quickly landed me a permanent role at one of the nation's largest financial institutions in an era of merger mania.

I enjoyed the collaboration and the challenges of integrating diverse organizations during mergers and acquisitions, availing me the opportunity for a series of promotions as well as a leading role in one of the industry's earliest diversity, equity, and inclusion initiatives. I leveraged the tuition-reimbursement program to complete my undergraduate degree before moving on to law school, while continuing to work full time between our Boston and Providence regional offices.

Moving to the Midwest after marrying, and accepting a C-suite role at another financial institution, my self-discipline eventually enabled me to eliminate those historical debts, to save the down payment for the purchase of our home, and to invest in my retirement. The birth of our daughter was immediately coupled with the establishment of her college savings fund. Each life decision was balanced on the three pillars of engendering financial literacy, employing a solid work ethic, and exercising self-discipline.

Even during those intentionally lean times of turning the financial corner, we traveled and enjoyed life, as we continue to do now. Each debt that was extinguished, including student loans and mortgages, simply led to increased cash flow with which to enjoy our amazing life more fully.

I haven't lost my work ethic or my self-discipline, but I have earned the peace of mind that comes with achieving financial security. I don't worry that a health scare, stock market dip, or global pandemic will leave me and my family destitute and living on the street. I live my amazing life with abundant resources that are the product of hard work, smart planning, and consistent self-discipline. Having been freed from the yoke of debt, I am able to enjoy my chosen vocation, volunteer activities, and family time without guilt.

I made just about every stupid financial mistake that a guy could make. Beside the personal satisfaction that I earned from honoring each of my ill-fated contractual commitments on my way to achieving financial security, I also have been able to effectively model fact-based financial literacy, a work ethic, and self-discipline to our daughter Elizabeth. As we'll discuss later regarding *Principle 10*, leaving a legacy requires more than simply money.

Taking Action: Achieving Financial Security To Win Your Amazing Life

You may be wondering why I have saved the financial principle to the end of the discussion.

While financial fitness is very important and mastering it will certainly ease the journey to living your best life, I wanted to ensure that the other critical principles did not get passed over after a fulsome discussion of finances.

I also hope that we can agree that money is not the solution to all of our issues. We've all met one or more persons who had financial abundance, but whose lives were a miserable mess. A jerk with money is still a jerk, and often a lonely jerk.

Our discussion about financial fitness isn't about becoming a zillionaire, but about achieving the financial peace of mind that will ease your journey as it has eased mine. And considering that I had made just about every dumb personal and professional financial mistake imaginable, if I could get *Principle 9* figured out in my life, then you'll surely outpace me. Perhaps you will become a zillionaire, if that is part of your overall life plan.

Even if you are currently financially very secure, maybe even overrun with abundance, it's a good idea to review the principle anyway. You may be able to guide someone else who continues to struggle with finances like I once did. You'll be an amazing role model for them. Either way, I recommend that you assess, plan, and execute your way to greater financial security.

Assess

We all start somewhere. I can recall a time in my life when my weekly grocery budget was ten dollars, my financial misdeeds had overwhelmed me, and I was working two jobs to pay off debts that included the deficiency balance on a repossessed vehicle.

At that point, the assessment process had already begun, because I had begun to accept the fact that I was in a deep financial hole. For me personally, declaring bankruptcy was not an option that I could morally undertake. I had incurred the debts willingly, no matter how stupidly or naively, so I knew that I remained responsible to fulfilling my commitments.

I had contracted to purchase the car on credit. I had eaten the restaurant meals and worn the department store clothing. I had consumed the beer. What sense was there in pretending that the debt was someone else's fault, when clearly it was my own actions that had gotten me into the situation that I then found myself in?

Assessing your financial starting point simply means to figure out how much income you have, how much outflow you have, what else do you need/want to purchase, and how far out of balance are you? You can do this in a computer spreadsheet, in a notebook, or on the back of an envelope. But do it.

You may not like the result of your self-assessment and you certainly won't help your cause by beating yourself up over the past, but you have to take this step before you can begin to plan.

Until you know where you stand, you have no way of knowing what direction to go and the steps to take to get you to where you need and want to be.

Plan

Depending upon where your self-assessment lands, your plan might begin very simply or it may welcome a complex multi-tiered solution.

I can recall when my plan included purchasing a mug at Starbucks so that I could get cheap refills every time I went there to study. I could sit in Starbucks for hours drinking coffee, staying warm, and getting ahead on my reading for college and law school classes.

My plan at one time included having two restaurant jobs simultaneously, so that I would be guaranteed two free or discounted hot meals on most days and I would be too busy to be able to go out to bars and spend more money at night.

These are not the plans of a Warren Buffett or a Ray Dalio, but represented the very simple baby steps that a streetwise guy like me could take at a time in my financial life when I was clawing my way out of a deep money pit. And before you begin thinking that steps like these certainly couldn't spur major financial shifts in one's life, consider that the core of these baby step principles eventually led me to fund higher education, purchase a home, and provide my family with the leisure experiences that they desired.

Baby steps work until bigger steps may be taken. In fact, I highly encourage that you build initial steps into your personal financial recovery plan that are so simple, you know in advance that you can achieve them. Why? Because you need to develop the habit of winning financially after succumbing to coming up short for so long.

Set yourself up to win on the small things, and pretty soon you will figure out strategies to win on bigger things. You'll figure out how to increase your income in a way that makes sense for you and your loved ones. You'll figure out how to reduce expenses and put more money toward reducing the principle on your debts, thereby further reducing how much you ultimately waste on interest. You'll figure out how to save enough money to treat your family to memorable experiences, paid in full, without incurring new debt.

Execute

When you've gotten honest with yourself about the state that you're in through a reliable financial self-assessment, and then have begun to detail the first steps of your personal financial recovery plan, you will now be ready to execute on a plan that will become so second-nature, you'll look back and wonder why you hadn't started performing these tactics sooner.

I have a lot of respect for many notable financial experts who have guided millions of people over the years. While often divergent in their approaches, ranging from the very conservative lean-livers to the more extravagant risk-taking you-only-live-once crowd, each has provided seeds of wisdom that can lead to financial recovery. My own journey adopted different seeds of wisdom depending upon where on the journey I found myself. I planted quite a lush garden from those seeds, and have lived well off their fruit ever since.

Your financial recovery should incorporate the financial tactics that make the most sense to you and your situation at any given point in time. I recommend a few guidelines regardless of where you are in your recovery path.

☐ Build fun into the process at every stage.
☐ Continually strengthen the reserve.
☐ Optimize risk to increase rewards.

Build Fun Into The Process At Every Stage

Taking each one in turn, I start with fun. Fun takes on a two-fold purpose. You have to know *why* you are doing what you're doing, because in the beginning, it's going to **suck**. And you have to be able to have a little fun each day. Fun is the attitude to adopt to cheat Death.

Yes, being broke and in debt was already tough. But now that you are consciously owning up to your money pit and applying some self-discipline to improve your situation, it's going to feel painful for at least a little while longer.

Therefore, you've got to include a fun objective to which you can look forward to at some milestone. Perhaps you are going to take your family to the movies once every couple weeks or vacation at a waterpark next summer without taking on new debt.

But you also need a daily reinforcement of fun. For me, it was my mug of discounted Starbucks coffee. It could be a cheap gym membership. A bagel each morning. Netflix.

But regardless of what it is that gives you that daily shot of relaxation, don't try to forego all pleasure in the false belief that you can't afford it and that you'll somehow get out of debt sooner by spending that money on bills. Like a diet, trying to achieve 100% perfection in the short term is a recipe for failure in the long-term, because *everyone* needs an outlet to just be human. Remember the 90/10 plan that I described back in *Principle 3: Optimize Physical Health*? Well, you can apply it successfully to your financial recovery as well.

Continually Strengthen The Reserve

While this statement may appear directly contradictory to

what we just discussed above, you will always want to continu-ally strengthen your financial reserves. No matter how finan-cially secure you have or will become, do not fall into a habit of spending more than you are bringing in.

While your income, spending, and saving may fluctuate in the short-term, throughout the month or over the course of a few months (e.g. around the holidays or before an income tax refund arrives), you will want to develop the consistent habit of spend-ing less than your income over the rolling span of time. And, yes, that is still while allowing yourself the daily release of fun and the periodic milestone fun activities that you've built into your plan.

Why?

Because in the near term, you want to build up a financial re-serve to absorb the inevitable contingencies that will arise (e.g. need new tires, urgent care visit, job loss). For the longer term, you are building the fiscal discipline that will be required to fully fund your retirement savings and other investments. And you'll be building up that reserve while executing on your debt reduction strategy and paying your bills on time.

In the beginning, you may only be able to increase your reserve by a few dollars each week. Perhaps you begin purchasing gro-ceries that allow you to take your lunch and beverages to work, instead of purchasing lunch, snacks, and beverages from take-out restaurants and vending machines. But you will soon be able to spot additional dollars blowing away in the breeze and recapture them to redeploy some of them to pay down debts, while stowing some of them away in savings.

No one should have to skip a visit to the doctor. No one should drive on that donut tire for an extended period of time. No one should lose everything and go homeless when unexpected job loss occurs. Financial setbacks will happen. The time to plan is now. The time to execute is now. Own your financial recovery.

Optimize Risk To Increase Rewards

These *10 Thriving Life Principles* are interdependent. In no way am I suggesting in previous sections that you should be satisfied with a mediocre income. On the contrary, I can assure you that you will achieve financial security that will suit any definition of success that much faster if you can increase your income sooner than later. But, you had to take some smaller steps first before you could take on additional risk.

In other words, you haven't just been focused on improving your finances. You've also been making progress to reclaim the life you deserve to live--spiritually, physically, emotionally, etc.

Therefore, undertaking more risk financially is also a gradual and well-planned exercise. You candidly assessed your financial state and owned up to the prior decisions and habits that landed you in the rut. You committed to making necessary changes and developed a plan of achievable steps, likely involving lifestyle adjustments and new habits.

The result of these positive decisions has improved your physical and emotional health, reduced your stress, and given you a glimpse of all that you are capable of. And you're just getting started!

But also realize that each of these conscious decisions *you* made [to spend less, eat better, spend more time with uplifting people, and more] actually represented taking a *risk* each time. Even the smallest change, perhaps going to the bar less frequently, involved taking a risk—facing criticism for not hanging out, or being lonely—that you were willing to take for the bigger payoff of reclaiming the larger, fuller life that you *deserve*.

You built **fun** into the execution of your plan, even as you strengthened your financial reserve. These factors were not ends unto themselves, but stepping stones toward greater fulfillment. That's where the risk comes in, and optimizing your risk simply means getting the best outcome from your investment of time, effort, and money.

There are so many examples that you could give, so I'm going to choose a common one that people consult with me about—purchasing your first home.

Let's assume that you are either living with family or renting an apartment. You've been getting your financial outflow under control with new habits while still allowing yourself some affordable fun. You've been saving money, but it's not accumulating fast enough that it would provide you a down payment on a decent home any time this lifetime. What to do?

Think about what you *can* do to optimize your savings, and a number of things may come to mind. But let's assume that you've already reduced expenses as much as practical. What else can you do? Earn more income!

Think about what you can do to earn more income. Can you...

☐ Apply for a promotion at your current employer?
☐ Apply for a better-paying position at another employer?
☐ Take on a second job?
☐ Help your spouse or life partner to receive a promotion or better-paying position?
☐ Teach a class?
☐ Start a side business?
☐ Do something else that I haven't listed here?

There is no single right answer, because your personal employment situation will dictate a series of decisions that make the most sense *for you and your loved ones*. But the bottom line is that you can take control of your income-earning potential.

You may have to earn a new certification, move to another city, or be willing to work a different schedule.

Remember, in this example, we were seeking to increase the rate of savings for a down payment on a first home. Like many financial risks that you are willing to take, the short-term investment of your time and effort can dramatically increase the effectiveness of your execution on the strategy. And you are in control of that time and effort.

To reclaim the most amazing life you deserve, you want to optimize your financial health, keep fun in the picture, and take sensible risks to improve your situation in a manner that fulfills your objectives and dreams.

◆ ◆ ◆

Living Your Own Amazing Life

Now it's your turn to pause and take action. Invest a few minutes to reflect upon these questions and when you are ready, write your responses in your *Cheating Death: The 10 Thriving Life Principles Journal* or in a notebook.

1. As you think about your own financial journey, is there a pillar that you believe you need to strengthen to achieve financial security?

2. What are one or two top activities that you could begin to do or enjoy more often if you achieved financial security in your life?

3. When you achieve financial security, will you continue working in your current career or will you take yourself in a new direction of work, leisure, and volunteerism?

PRINCIPLE 10: DEFINE YOUR LEGACY

"Live, Love, Laugh, Leave a Legacy"

~ STEPHEN R. COVEY[17]

E verything that we have received in life is a gift. Life itself is the most precious gift.

Think about that for a moment. From the very miracle of our birth to the last breath that we will one day inhale, we have received life without any action on our part.

Time is one of life's greatest dividends of all. Ask a man in hospice what he would give for more time with his spouse or his children. Or the business traveler whose delayed flight will cause her to miss her child's soccer game. We are inclined to spend our time with those people we love, even when external obligations pull us in many different directions.

We are hardwired to give back to others what has so freely been given to us. Often that innate impulse to give can be suppressed by other seemingly more urgent matters. For so many years, I made excuses when I could have been making a differ-

ence. Although I had grown up participating in volunteer activities, when I became mired in my own emotional and financial missteps, I became increasingly selfish and my giving spirit
faded. I fell short of the mark.

What Does It Mean To Define Your Legacy?

As with each of *The 10 Thriving Life Principles*, *Principle 10* operates interdependently with each of the remaining principles.
Yet it also naturally follows the preceding principles upon
which it is most securely based. Defining one's legacy is a natural outgrowth of a life well planned and well lived, as a woman
or man must possess some degree of substance and stability to
provide meaningful sustenance to those individuals whom she
or he would wish to uplift.

That is not to say that you have to have mastered each principle before you can begin to define your legacy. But defining one's legacy is made significantly more effective when the
foundational principles have been matured through formative
experience.

You can't give what you yourself don't possess. But if you don't
plan to give it all away, then you won't fully cheat Death. Anything that you leave on the table will pass with you, and it may
not pass to the benefit of whom you would have otherwise directed it be distributed.

Your legacy speaks to the truth of who you are and how you
have lived your own life (*Principle 1*), and embodies a selflessness that reflects the spiritual peace that has come to elevate
your consciousness (*Principle 2*). Your legacy represents the
very tangible expression of your love that you will extend to
others in your family and your broader community in perpetu-
ity long after you have met the inevitable.

Your legacy requires of you that you have the stamina to endure the longevity that a productive life requires (*Principle 3*), and that you have applied and added to your God-given talents through constructive and practical education and training (*Principle 4*).

Your legacy recognizes that your earthly victories matter only when they are born of healthy love and forgiveness (*Principle 5*), and undertaken and celebrated with those women and men, girls and boys, to whom you have dedicated your life and without whom your labors and investments would not have true meaning (*Principle 6*).

Your legacy takes on a life of its own when it spills over into your local, national, and global community to uplift the lives of those who may require a helping hand, not so unlike the helping hand that was extended to us in our own brokenness (*Principle 7*). From the smallest act of unbiased kindness to the most authoritative expressions that you can muster to advocate on behalf of others based solely upon their superior merit, diverse experience, and boundless potential, you can extend your legacy across a millennium (*Principle 8*) in ways that you will not live to see.

Your legacy will certainly take on a greater dimension if you can underwrite it with an outpouring of your own financial success (*Principle 9*), but again I must emphasize that one's legacy is as much about **time** and **substance** as it is about money. A legacy delivers its impact when other people are compelled to carry forth your vision of a better tomorrow and devote *their* time and attention to cementing that vision into meaningful action.

How I Came To Define My Legacy

Like each of the preceding nine principles, I am still learning, still growing in my mastery of *Principle 10*. I will go to my grave still trying to perfect my legacy. That's okay with me, because

I am committed to helping women and men, girls and boys, old and young, black and white, and more, achieve their most amazing lives.

My own amazing life has been the dividend of so many selfless legacies imparted upon me since childhood and up through this very day. I did not rise up due to privilege, and yet I am privileged to be able to give back to future generations.

I am compelled to live each day fully, giving back to others, because family members, educators, community volunteers, corporate executives, and others were willing to give of their time, wisdom, and financial resources to uplift me.

I came to define my legacy from an early age when all I had to give was my time and my heart. As I grew in knowledge and experience, I was able to share skills and education with youth in classrooms and athletic venues. I have been able to reduce hunger, provide access to clean drinking water, beautify impoverished neighborhoods, and share the good news of our Creator around the globe. Sometimes I am delivering upon my legacy with my own hands, but oftentimes it is delivered through the hands of others who have committed their lives to perfecting a niche of selflessness locally, nationally, and across the continents.

I came to accept that I cannot do all things, but that I can do *something*. I refused to be constrained by limitations of time or other resources, and instead have allowed my compassion to become the multiplier. Together, with you, we can ensure that our lives will have made a difference long before we meet the Inevitable at a future intersection.

Taking Action: Defining Your Legacy To Win Your Amazing Life

I encourage you to pause for a moment and ask yourself if you have been acting like the giver that you were born to be. This may be an area of your life where you already excel, and if that's the case, then I tip my cap to you for the impact that you are already having to improve the lives of others.

I know that I fell short of this so many times in my own life, and have engaged in much soul searching over the years. I have dialogued with many others struggling to define their own legacy, and some of those struggles may resonate with you as well.

All giving is good

"Cris, I feel real bad, but I can't afford to contribute to my company's toy & coat drive. Still eating ramen, but my student loan payment just kicked in, on top of rent and utilities...what can I do?"

Oh yeah, I've been there. Holiday cheer quickly turns to holiday fear. No one wants to be that one person looking stingy. Especially if you, like me, received the kindness of strangers in your own childhood home.

You're NOT alone. No matter how busy your new career, you have an asset to give: TIME. Those same organizations seeking monetary donations on Facebook and Instagram will gladly accept a donation of YOU.

Pay it forward. Lift up vulnerable youth & families when you share your time with Big Brothers Big Sisters of America, UNCF, Junior Achievement, and more. Not just during this holiday season, but year-round.

Just chill. In due time, you'll assist non-profit boards and write gala checks. But at this financially lean phase of your journey, focus on generously giving the Time portion, and defer the Talent & Treasure...for now. Our Lord measures them equally.

Breaking bread

You've heard it said that "there's no such thing as a free lunch".

I beg to differ. Food security was often an issue in my earlier life, so I both treasured the opportunity to donate food for the benefit of others, but to also partake of events where food would be served.

I still prefer directly *participating* in charitable events over simply making a financial contribution. Whether attending a brunch or dinner event, or preparing a meal for families in need, food continues to be central to stewardship. There's always a sense of kinship when you sit down sweaty and hungry with your fellow volunteers to share food and drink after you've spent the day painting a school or raking yards for the disabled.

At a more practical level as a financially-strapped teenager and young adult, I quickly learned that all volunteer opportunities came with some form of sustenance. Whether it was fruit and bagels at a morning event, pizza at mid-day, or left-over turkey and mashed potatoes after serving homeless Thanksgiving guests, I knew that I could count on receiving some form of sustenance for my investment of time.

I hear some of you judging me, as in "hey, you're supposed to give without expecting anything in return". But I also see others of you nodding your head, understanding *precisely* what I mean.

At a time in my life when my meager budget led me to consider breaded meat byproducts from the budget grocery store as the protein source in my basket, a free meal following a day devoted to volunteering was sometimes the healthiest meal of my day.

The point is that if you are giving fully of your heart, your skills, and your time to assist others, there is nothing wrong with enjoying the gastric goodness that accompanies the volunteer opportunity.

Role models

*"Cris, I'm not sure that my participation is really making
a difference."*

Oh, my friend, I can *assure* you that your participation is making a difference.

I can't go back and thank all the countless individuals who have made a difference in my own life, simply because they invested their time, talent, or treasure into me. I can tell you that each of them formed a guide wire of hope that allowed me to escape the economic, educational, and emotional challenges of my youth.

Classroom volunteers. Sports coaches. Career day speakers. Food pantry donors and volunteers. And more. Every single one of them led me to return years later to step into their shoes and provide that same ray of hope to another young person, another family in need.

Don't wait to be asked. Even if you don't sense the need, your very presence is exactly what is needed. Some young person is thirsty to see a successful woman or man come to their school, their team, their church, their community center. A woman or man that looks like them, sounds like them, struggled like them, dreamt like them.

You don't have to be a billionaire entrepreneur, an Olympic athlete, or an elected official to share your legacy. For those of us who needed to know that we could survive the shame of poverty, escape the bullies, kick the addictions, graduate high school, find a vocation...we needed someone just like YOU.

I've seen people bring farming, equestrian lessons, and golf to the inner city. I've seen people bring coding, theatre, and scholarships to rural villages. There is at least one experience, one skill, one open door that you can share that will mean everything to that youth or family who dreams of a better tomorrow.

Like seeds that will one day grow into saplings that will later tower above the forest, your presence will impregnate hidden talents whose outcomes you will likely never know. Show up anyway.

Writing checks

As you enjoy increased financial success, the time will come when you will be able to donate substantial money to the causes you wish to support. Perhaps you are already doing that.

As we've discussed throughout this chapter, please don't let your financial contributions *replace* your time investments. Yes, as any development officer will tell you, financial donations are *critical* to the success of any worthy not-for-profit organization. But your money should simply be a complement to your time and talent.

Look at all that you have achieved in life! Those children, those families are never going to see your individual donation. They are not going to celebrate your automatic contribution, your check, or your tithe. But they will embrace you in a grateful hug, trade a fist bump, or exchange a tearful smile so long as you keep showing up.

Certainly, purchase the gala tickets and enjoy a night out on the town with the ones you love, your friends, and your professional colleagues. And also make sure that you don't lose physical contact with the very human beings or four-legged friends for whom you are making those contributions.

Sometimes it gets too easy to give financially and figure that is all that is needed. But in addition to those in need of your organization's assistance, so too does that next generation of volunteers need to know that the old guard hasn't outgrown the mission.

Giving is a three-legged stool. So, by all means, give generously of your treasure, but do so in concert with your time and talent. To whom much has been given, from them much will be expected. When you give of your time, talent and treasure to uplift others, then you have successfully cheated Death. That next generation thanks you for your stewardship.

Living Your Own Amazing Life

Now it's your turn to pause and take action. Invest a few minutes to reflect upon these questions and when you are ready, write your responses in your *Cheating Death: The 10 Thriving Life Principles Journal* or in a notebook.

1. Describe one of two events in your own life when you were the beneficiary of someone else's selfless legacy. What positive difference did those events make in your own life?

2. At this phase of your life, what are one or two methods by which you can contribute your time, talent, or treasure to uplift others in your local community?

3. As you think about meeting the inevitable end of your life (perhaps decades from now), how would you like your legacy memorialized when others speak about the substantial impact that you had upon improving the lives of others?

GET BACK UP AGAIN

"...[Y]ou should never, ever be embarrassed by those struggles. You should never view your challenges as a disadvantage. Instead, it's important for you to understand that your experience facing and overcoming adversity is actually one of your biggest advantages."

~ MICHELLE OBAMA[18]

You and I have stepped through *The 10 Thriving Life Principles* together for what I hope will be the first of many times. I've candidly acknowledged throughout our discussion that I made a lot of mistakes along the way of discerning the principles in my own life. Furthermore, I gladly admit that I remain a student of these principles, even as I aid others daily to practice the principles in their own lives.

I remind you that if a screw-up like me has been able to overcome adversity to cheat Death on multiple occasions, and to live my most amazing life, then you are certainly far better equipped to achieve *your* most amazing life more quickly and less clumsily than I did.

At no point along my journey have I ever fooled myself into thinking that I have it all figured out. More importantly, I faced setbacks along the way. Sometimes when the momentum was moving forward in my direction, I would say something, do something, or even *fail* to do something that would stall the momentum.

Self-sabotage? Immaturity? Stubbornness? Who knows!

I got back up, dusted myself off, and sought to pick up where I had left off.

And so will you. If you ain't dead, then get the heck back up and get after it!

Each day we must love ourselves enough to get back up and start again. By extension, we must also love others enough to lend a hand and a kind word to support them as they get back up and start again. We're all in this together.

Simply by traveling this far through the entire *10 Thriving Life Principles* with me, you have already begun to practice them in your own life.

On many days, you will make forward progress on one or more principles, in small ways and in larger ways.

On some days, you will climb into bed feeling like you didn't make any forward progress, but upon further reflection, you'll realize that you didn't slip back either.

And on some days, perhaps several in a row, you will find yourself sinking in the quicksand of life, pulled down by the negative self-talk, destructive habits, or toxic people that you are striving to leave behind.

I know each of these conditions to be true, because I have experienced all three. I learned not to let the highs get too high, or the lows too low. Even when I slipped backward for several days in a row, I held tightly to my vision of the amazing life. I refused to let go of the timeless principles that I knew would lead me beyond my past mistakes and allow me to achieve my dreams. I continued to get back up again so that I could cheat Death.

You can't allow the setbacks to become your put backs. Nobody can put you back on the shelf except you, and that will happen only if you give up on yourself and quit. And if you quit, then it's "game over" and Death wins.

It's perfectly acceptable for you to turn the lights out, climb under the covers, and call it a day. You can reduce the impact of the downward slide, and finish in neutral for the day. But you must NEVER lose sight of tomorrow, because when you receive the blessing that is tomorrow, you must be ready to re-engage with *The 10 Thriving Life Principles* in your own life.

Remember, we're all just outrunning the inevitable. But we weren't created to go through a daily Hell. We're not promised one more day, so when we do receive the gift of one more day, we've got an obligation to optimize our forward progress.

Not sure where to turn?

Turn back to the beginning of this book. Or turn to your favorite parts. Or turn to the principle that is causing you the current challenge and review your responses in your journal to the questions at the end of the chapter. Or turn to the principle that is your easiest to practice, and just keep practicing it.

Just. Do. Something.

You're going to live your own amazing life. That's settled. The question is: how long do you want to take to achieve it?

When we meet in person or virtually, I want to hear all about the amazing life that you have achieved, the journey that you took to get there, and the insights that you have gained along the way. But I'm also going to want to hear about the adversity that you have overcome, because I know firsthand that nothing worthwhile in this life is ever achieved without overcoming some adversity.

I am so proud of you for making this commitment to yourself and to your loved ones. I have shared my love for you through the pages of this book. And I am wholly confident that you will **live the rest of your life as the *BEST* of your life!**

Living Your Own Amazing Life

Now it's your turn to pause and take action. Invest a few minutes to reflect upon these questions and when you are ready, write your responses in your *Cheating Death: The 10 Thriving Life Principles Journal* or in a notebook.

1. Make a list of the negative self-talk, destructive habits, or toxic people that have the greatest potential to set you back on your journey to achieve your most amazing life. What steps will you take today to separate yourself from those potential setbacks?

2. Which of *The 10 Thriving Life Principles* has been (or may be) the most difficult one for you to master? What can you do today to capture a small win with that principle?

3. Which of *The 10 Thriving Life Principles* has been (or may be) the easiest for you to master? How can you leverage that easier principle to carry you through some of the challenges you will face along your journey?

WINNING YOUR AMAZING LIFE, FULLY LIVED

"Do the difficult things while they are easy and do the great things while they are small. A journey of a thousand miles must begin with a single step."

~ LAO TZU[19]

W ell, it's been a heck of a stroll together. But it ain't over yet.

You and I have journeyed through *Cheating Death: The 10 Thriving Life Principles* together for the first time (or perhaps a subsequent refresher). You're already further along your personal path to winning YOUR amazing life than you were when we first got together.

I've been upfront with you the entire time, that I don't have it all figured out yet. I'm on this journey with you to this very day. But I am confident, based on my own experience, that you will love the way your own life will continue to improve as you make the incremental shifts that each of *The 10 Thriving Life Principles* suggests.

You're already further along with some of the principles, while possibly just exploring the contours of other principles. That's the beauty of *The 10 Thriving Life Principles*! You can focus your attention day by day, even hour by hour, on those principles that most appeal to your energy and needs at that time. Progress is progress.

Identifying Your Why

You've learned a little bit about how I chose to cheat Death and to live my life fully. You see that even a guy like me who came from nothing, made it worse, and then somehow managed to make it into something great, could eventually win before it was too late.

But my life isn't *your* life and my motivations aren't *your* motivations. It's your turn now. It truly is all about YOU!

You've got to identify your own "why".

You may already know who or what "it" is, or at least have some suspicion. It's likely something that's been nagging at you for a while. And with each passing day it grows within you. You sense that the inevitable moves one day closer to you each day that you delay.

That feeling, it isn't going to go away. Like hunger. Or love. You can try to suppress it to a "more appropriate" time, but it's not going to disappear.

Bear in mind, every day you live, you are one day closer to the inevitable. Death moves in on you moment by moment that you delay. Not being morbid, just stating a fact.

So, you're either going to get up each day living the life that *you* have chosen, or you will set aside your chosen life and continue to grind for someone else's dream. Either way, you have made a choice.

> Choose a life fully lived. Choose to live your own amazing life. Choose love to cheat Death.

> Choose to spend your time with the people you love doing the things you enjoy doing with one another. When the end comes, you don't get the opportunity to cash in all that "banked" time you spent at work.

> Choose to spend your money serving the causes that you most value, both for pleasure and for promoting humankind. You certainly can't take it with you to the hereafter.

My life isn't your life. Your buddy's life isn't your life. Your boss's life *certainly* isn't your life. This is on you. *You've* got to step up. *You've* got to decide.

The point is that you have to identify the who, what, and why that you would enjoy each day if you could spend your time and money how you please.

Banishing Fear

> *"Cris, what if I'm not ready...or I do this and it doesn't work...or my mother-in-law calls me a lazy bum...or...or..."*

So what? You've been dealing with some or all of those thoughts your entire life. Are you living for your self-actualization and your immediate family's destiny...or are you living to please other people in the neighborhood, at work, in you extended family?

Put another way, those are fears that you've allowed to slow you down in the past. We all have early childhood memories of someone putting us down or making fun of us for doing something less than perfectly.

We then spent the rest of our lives reliving those moments, viscerally experiencing the burning sensation of embarrassment for a dropped fly ball or fashion fail. Maybe you peed yourself in kindergarten or vomited on your date in college. So what?!

Truth is that the only reason those events continue to feed our fear of failure is that we willingly power those fears. Oh, it may be an unconscious fuel line, but it's still a product of our own self-doubt.

That kid who laughed at your for missing that shot? That popular girl who led her clique to sneer at your self-made fashion statement? They don't even remember your name. So why are you still recalling some event that lasted 10 seconds five or thirty years ago?

Like President Franklin Delano Roosevelt spoke to a nationwide early-20th century audience gripped by uncertainty, "The only thing we have to fear is fear itself."[20]

You *might* fail. But if you do the things we will discuss in a moment, I believe **you will succeed**.

And if you don't initially succeed, then hopefully the examples of recovering from total screw-ups that I've provided will enable you to pick yourself up and go after success again. Failing won't result in failure, but quitting on yourself sure will. And quitting is simply an open invitation for Death to claim victory over you.

Crafting A Framework

If you were going on a family vacation in six months, you wouldn't just forget about it until the morning of departure. You'd think about it, talk about it, gather information, make reservations at your destination, and make arrangements for someone to watch your home and pets.

Stepping out into your own chosen life will follow a similar path. You picked up this book, because you knew that you deserved something more fulfilling than what you already had. You traveled through the chapters with me, because you had already been thinking about it, likely beginning to talk about it.

I like to let my hair down and see where life takes me. Despite what many people have told me about their perception of me as carefree and spontaneous, I live a rather risk-averse and carefully planned lifestyle. Before I stepped out into my own life fully lived, I had identified my who, my what, and my why.

The how became the framework for determining when it would make sense to retire.

o Because we would not yet be at the legal retirement age to draw cash flow from pension, retirement account, or Social Security benefits, we prioritized liquidating our outstanding debts.
o We invested in quality improvements to our properties to ensure maximum useful life of all systems and features.
o We built a solid backstop of tangible investments from which we could draw passive income.
o We identified a variety of vocations that would fulfill us spiritually, mentally, and emotionally from which we would continue to earn a stream of income for travel, leisure, necessities like food and health insurance, and incidentals.

And we did these things over a span of years while raising a family, traveling, tithing, and enjoying a comfortable lifestyle. You've got to continue to optimize each phase of the journey, even before you make the leap.

Building the framework simply requires a vision of where you want to go, and taking steps each day to move closer to the objectives. Some days you go farther than others. Other days, you need to put a new roof on the house and your framework construction hits the pause button.

Your blueprint is the key. No matter what happens each day, you **always keep your eye on the prize**. Moving forward while others are wasting time, wasting money, wasting away. We didn't get here by accident, and neither will you.

Accepting Uncertainty

"Cris, what if I go through all the planning, make the leap, and it doesn't work?!"

It might not work the first time. Everyone's situation is different, from the planning to the execution to the unexpected contingencies that may arise at the most inconvenient of times. It worked for us, and it works for most. But all I have shared is my journey.

Many climbers attempt Mount Everest. Few reach the summit. Some die on the ascent. An even greater number die on the descent. People keep climbing Everest.

Life is full of uncertainty. But I made a decision that I'd rather accept uncertainty on my own terms, rather than succumb to the siren song of seeming security that would slowly suck my time and attention away from the people, places, and activities that I yearn to enjoy during my relatively short time here on Earth.

Those who choose to climb Everest know that they are not promised a fixed life span. They climb anyway.

You have not been promised a fixed life span. Do you want to spend it keeping up with the Joneses or do you want to spend it keeping up with your grandchildren while they are still young?

I accepted that the worst-case scenario wasn't even a bad scenario. If I had planned poorly, then I would simply reintegrate myself into my profession for some period of time and recalibrate our financial position.

Living my life fully was never about 'accumulating things' or 'flashy living'. It was always about soaking up as much time enjoying the people, places, and activities that I love. I've never been disappointed in the decision that I made.

And, I suspect, neither will you or your loved ones.

Going For It – Choose The Date

"Cris, how do I know when the right time will arrive to go?"

You'll just know. And you'll likely feel a bit giddy about it. Perhaps a little smug, too.

Somehow you cracked the code. You figured out the who, the why, and the what that would make you stop subjecting yourself to the daily grind, whether on the factory floor or in the corporate suite. You set to work patiently building a framework according to your balanced blueprint.

Then one day you are looking at your loved ones, having already reviewed your account balances, and you just know.

Because this was never about feeling aggrieved, or being pissed off at anyone, the actual announcement at work is rather transactional. You follow whatever is the appropriate protocol to formally submit your retirement and you go back to your daily work.

You may have chosen a span of a month or more, to ensure that your replacement can be selected and fully trained. You may be asked to stay on even longer in your current capacity and offered a retention bonus or a consulting gig. You will have to decide if that arrangement squares with your immediate post-retirement plans (including planned celebratory travel), but more than likely you'll be able to find a mutually-beneficial accommodation.

You will then enjoy casual conversations with co-workers, some of whom will be curious to know what you plan to do next and how you managed to retire at your early age.

If, like me, you've chosen to transition to some form of service to the community, a few may question why you would have given up the 'security' of your position, salary, and benefits to do something not-for-profit.

It's inconceivable to some people that your decision is premised on fully living the intangibles of life, rather than grind fearfully day after day for a long-sought financial hereafter that may last decades...or less than a year.

It really doesn't matter what anyone else thinks. Remember, it's YOUR life.

Don't Over Plan The Future

So, now what?

Take it one day at a time. Unless you've immediately undertaken fixed commitments, you can meet each hour, each day, each week as it comes.

Time has become your currency. Donate it, invest it, spend it, but above all, don't waste another minute of it.

As I shared in my story with you, I got a 'late' start, and yet somehow I managed to come out all right in the deal.

You might be younger or older than I was, but either way, it really doesn't matter. **You have cheated Death.** You are alive and you are spending time doing what you want, when you want, with the people you love.

You come to discover that the beach, the lake, the golf course, and the museums are far less crowded during the week than they were on the weekends.

I look forward to seeing you there!

Now, go **live the rest of your life as the BEST of your life**!

Living Your Own Amazing Life

Now it's your turn to pause and take action. Invest a few minutes to reflect upon these questions and when you are ready, write your responses in your *Cheating Death: The 10 Thriving Life Principles Journal* or in a notebook.

1. Describe two or three of the amazing activities that you will engage in when you break free of your past restraints. Who are the people that you will share those activities with?

2. Who are the special people in your family, your circle of friends, and your community that would benefit from applying *The 10 Thriving Life Principles* to more fully realize their own amazing lives? What small step can you take today to share this opportunity with those special people?

3. What date have you chosen to break free? How will you break the news? How will you celebrate that last day of your former life?

AFTERWORD

T hank you for sharing this part of the journey with me.

No matter where you are on the life path, simply by picking up this book, you have already demonstrated that you are on your way. As I said to you in the beginning, this isn't a get-rich-quick thing—it's a living an amazing life fully thing. It's a love thing.

No amount of money replaces the hours spent with your husband or wife building a life together.

No amount of authority or prominence at work replaces hours spent sitting on the floor playing games with your daughters and sons.

No latest technology gadget, fancy vehicle, or over-mortgaged home is going to enable you to build a clean drinking water facility to improve the health of a village in an underdeveloped nation.

You've always had an inner sense of who you were truly created to be. I only came along to help you realize that there is a path to follow to allow yourself to rise up and be that person sooner than later.

When you live life fully for all the days that remain for you here on Earth, others live life fully with you. Family, old friends, new friends, and friends that you haven't even met yet. I look forward to being among those new friends whom you'll meet.

LET'S KEEP IN TOUCH

T hank you for joining me on this incredible journey to explore *The 10 Thriving Life Principles* together.

And the journey does not end here. You have an amazing opportunity to strengthen yourself in each of the principles daily. One of the best ways to do that is to share *The 10 Thriving Life Principles* with others.

Sharing *The 10 Thriving Life Principles* with the special people in your family, your friend circle, and your community demonstrates your love for them. Sharing will allow them to begin to more fully realize their own amazing lives. Imagine the impact that you can have on other women and men—especially if it is your intention to spend more time with those special people doing the amazing activities that you have planned.

Don't go it alone! From cruising the Caribbean or Mediterranean Seas to golfing on every day that ends in "Y", it's so much easier to enjoy your amazing life when those special people have also infused their own lives with an active practice of *The 10 Thriving Life Principles*.

There are many simple ways to share this opportunity with those special people and others in your local, national, or global community.

☐ Give copies of *Cheating Death: The 10 Thriving Life Principles* and the companion *Journal* to family members, friends, employees, faith-based groups, and community leaders.

☐ Engage your book club to read and discuss *Cheating Death: The 10 Thriving Life Principles* (or start a book club, and begin with *The 10 Thriving Life Principles*).

☐ Host a *10 Thriving Life Principles* discussion at work, at church, or within a community organization to which you belong.

☐ Invite me to engage in a live discussion and Q&A at your book club, your workplace, your school, your church, or your local community organization. We can tailor a discussion to one or more of *The 10 Thriving Life Principles* to align with key outcomes that your team or organization seek to achieve. [E-mail me at: outrunning.the.inevitable@gmail.com]

☐ Send me your own stories that describe your new insights, suggestions, victories, and challenges that you encounter as you apply *The 10 Thriving Life Principles* in your own life. With your permission included with your submission, I will gladly share your stories during live events, in blog posts, and in future publications. [Email me at: outrunning.the.inevitable@ gmail.com]

☐ Your own unique ways of sharing *The 10 Thriving Life Principles*.

It is my sincere hope that we do, in fact, get to meet one day. I look forward to sitting down and visiting with you, while you share your success story with me.

Until then, by God's grace, we'll keep outrunning the inevitable and cheating Death together.

END NOTES

Death in the Middle Ages

1. Hart, Kevin and Strauss, Neil. *I Can't Make This Up: Life Lessons*. New York. Simon & Shuster, 2017.

2. "A millennium of health improvement", BBC News, December 27, 1998, http://news.bbc.co.uk/2/hi/health/241864.stm (viewed May 16, 2020).

3. Life Expectancy, United States Centers for Disease Control and Prevention, https://www.cdc.gov/nchs/fastats/life-expectancy.htm(viewed May 16,2020).

Just Don't Die

4. "Jesus, Take the Wheel", written by Brett James, Hillary Lindsey and Gordie Sampson; recorded by Carrie Underwood; released October 2005; Sony/ATV Music Publishing.

The Promise and the Paradox

5. "It's My Life", written and produced by Jon Bon Jovi, Richie Sambora, and Max Martin, and co-produced by Luke Ebbin, *Crush* (2000).

Principle 1: Speak Your Truth

6. Ferguson, Don. Disney's *The Lion King*. [United States]: Mouse Works, 1994. Print.

7. Plato., & Jowett, B. (1937). *The dialogues of Plato*. New York: Random House.

Principle 2: Accept Spiritual Peace

8. "Serenity Prayer", attributed to Reinhold Niebuhr (1892-1971).

Principle 3: Optimize Physical Health

9. Kennedy, John F., "The Soft American", *Sports Illustrated*, vol. 13,

issue 26, pp. 14 – 17, December 26, 1960, Los Angeles, CA, Time, Inc., [viewed at http://www.recreatingwithkids.com/news/read-it-here-kennedys-the-soft-american/, May 17, 2020].

Principle 4: Feed Your Intellect

10. Attributed to Aristotle, [viewed at https://www.goodreads.com/quotes/95080-educating-the-mind-without-educating-the-heart-is-no-education, May 17, 2020].

Principle 5: Embrace Emotional Bliss

11. Karnazes, Dean. "Running is about finding your inner peace, and so is a life well lived." *Daily running log with weekly note*, Penguin Random, September 25, 2019.

Principle 6: Cherish Your Family

12. Bush, Barbara. *Speech of Nominee Spouse.* Republican National Convention, Houston, TX, August 19, 1992.

Principle 7: Expand Your Community

13. Day, Dorothy & Berrigan, Daniel. *The Long Loneliness: The Autobiography of the Legendary Catholic Social Activist.* Harper & Row. 1952, p. 285.

14. Myers-Briggs Type Indicator, [viewed at https://www.myersbriggs.org/my-mbti-personality-type/mbti-basics/, May 31, 2020].

Principle 8: Extend Opportunity Equitably

15. Angelou, Maya. *Wouldn't Take Nothing for My Journey Now.* New York: Random House, 1993.

Principle 9: Achieve Financial Security

16. Rand, Ayn. *Atlas Shrugged.* New York: Random House, 1957.

Principle 10: Define Your Legacy

17. Covey, Stephen R. *The 7 Habits of Highly Effective People: Restoring the Character Ethic.* New York: Free Press, 1989.

Get Back Up Again

18. Obama, Michelle, "Remarks by the First Lady at City College of New York Commencement", Office of the First Lady, Obama White House Archives, June 3, 2016. [Viewed at https://obamawhitehouse.archives.gov/the-press-

office/2016/06/03/remarks-first-lady-city-college-new-york-commencement, June 6, 2020.]

Winning Your Amazing Life, Fully Lived

19. Laozi, . and Stephen Mitchell. *Tao Te Ching: A New English Version*. New York, N.Y: Harper & Row, 1988.

20. Roosevelt, Franklin D. (Franklin Delano), 1882-1945. *Franklin D. Roosevelt's Inaugural Address of 1933*. Washington, DC: National Archives and Records Administration, 1988.

ACKNOWLEDGEMENT

My amazing life has been and continues to be one heck of a journey.

While I'm lucky simply to be alive, I'm even more fortunate to have met and been aided by so many selfless individuals along the way. In seeking to acknowledge these many women and men, I will undoubtedly fail to name so many more. I beg for your forgiveness in advance, as the lack of your inclusion along with many whom might have counted themselves obviously central to my success is not mistaken by you or them, but merely a glaring oversight on my part.

I invite you and those individuals not here included to send forth your names to me, so that I may ensure that you are explicitly added in a subsequent republication. Mention of the significant individuals below does not imply their agreement with or endorsement of any content included in this book, except where explicitly noted elsewhere.

So, where does one begin when so many have been so caring and instrumental?

As should have been evident throughout the preceding chapters, my very life centers around my beautiful bride Kimberly and our inspiring daughter Elizabeth, without whom I might not have sought to fully live my most amazing life.

My father, Council Anderson Mattoon, and my mother Jean Evelyn (Cicack) Mendoza gave me not only life, but abundant lifetimes of love and attention in the best way that they knew how. My stepmother Robin (Colvin) Wiggins demonstrated a lifetime of genuine love and taught me by her own example how to take more risks and to turn disappointment into determination and joy.

My maternal grandmother, Esther Kraft Cicack, exhibited a strength borne out of the Great Depression to overcome a mid-life stroke and move across the country with her family in her widowhood to start anew. My maternal grandfather, Walter Cicack, and his son, my uncle, of the same name, lived out ethical public service careers in the New York City Police Department and as Catholic men amidst challenging cultural shifts.

My paternal grandfather, Douglas Mattoon, for whom my brother is named, and my paternal grandmother (Gertrude) Mildred "Millie" Mattoon, lived amazing lives devoted to one another and to their children, forged by youthful emergence from the Great Depression that led to a lifetime of world exploration and cross-cultural acceptance well ahead of their times and standing in society. My uncle Matthew (Duff) Mattoon and aunt Victoria Wooters, who modeled for me that continued embrace of Millie & Doug's lust for this amazing life from their home in Westchester County, New York, that covered the expanse of New York City and the globe. My uncle Trow Mattoon and now-departed aunt Barbara Mattoon, of Brooklyn, New York, whose love and devotion to one another and others overlaid any struggles that their humble existence may have caused them.

Moving beyond members of the family from which I hailed, I can only scratch the surface of the multitude that further uplifted me, guided me, propelled me to drink deeply of this amazing life. Major Shepherd-El and Black Bottom Bred Publishing for believing in my vision. Steve Zenofsky, best friend made in second grade at Providence Street School in West Warwick, Rhode Island and best man in my wedding, who led me into and shared a lifelong devotion to Tony Robbins and all that is possible with directed attention and action focused on specific goals and objectives.

Through middle school and high school in Rhode Island, I was blessed to be befriended by so many, including Principal George Finch, and classmates Michelle (Chase) Frazier, Chris Plympton, Rich Anderson, and Tom Guzulaitis.

My transition to Houston in the eleventh grade was made smoother by Cross Country Coach Andy Ferrara, and team mates David Hall, Will Sakson, Peter Spong, Kevin Broussard, and Del Wilcoxson whom I met before the season even began. My time there was further improved by Bradley Rex, Brian Krumnow, Mike Romano, and many more.

Academically, I am indebted to Mrs. Elaine Edwards, my seventh grade English teacher, who pushed me to be better than I was allowing myself to be academically, even as I pushed back against her as an ungrateful scoundrel of an emotionally hurting child. Mrs. Beverly Greeney, my twelfth grade English teacher, who capitalized on the foundation laid by Mrs. Edwards, to engage me both in the intellectually stimulating buffet of Advanced Placement Literature, as well as to encourage me to compete in University Interscholastic League Ready Writing, of which I had previously been unaware and for which I would earn a State of Texas medal.

I am thankful for Texas A&M University, its Summer Orientation Program and Fish Camp, each of which extended to me the hand of welcome as I entered the University, and later afforded me world-class leadership opportunities as counselor and co-chair. Jody Manier and Suzanne Franks, who elevated the enjoyment and intellectual dialogue of being a university student. The Eta Upsilon Chapter of the Sigma Chi Fraternity at Texas A&M University, and specifically Dr. Ed Silverman who came to my assistance when I returned to school there in my own stutter-step attempt to rebuild my life in my early twenties.

My law school years at Roger Williams University in Bristol, Rhode Island were enhanced by distinguished faculty and administrators, especially Bruce Kogan, Michael Yelnosky, Matthew Harrington, Larry Ritchie, Jonathan Gutoff, Anthony Santoro, and Linda Vieira who each challenged me and led me to love the study and practice of the law even more than I thought I could. Fellow students Larry Signore, Dena Castricone, David Dolbashian, John Catterall, and Katy Hynes were integral to my law school experience for all the right reasons.

Professionally, my entrepreneurial path was cleared by Rhode Island women and men genuinely interested in giving me a shot to prove myself, notably Thayden Waltonen, John Byrne, and the Mishnock Grove. In the restaurant business that launched me into sales and management, I fondly recall Roman (Grandy's, Houston, Texas), Sammy (Bennigan's, College Station, Texas), and Dennis Garside (Chili's, Warwick, Rhode Island) for their encouragement.

At the risk of surely failing to name so many important contributors to my further professional development in public accounting, financial services, and the law, I recall fondly for their mentorship and advocacy Phil Baker (Battle Mountain Gold); Bob Nasiatka, Lionel Harnois, Peter Flanagan, Maria Leonard, Robert Pirri, and Pedro Ferrara (FleetBoston); Michael Poulos and Janet Ososki (Michigan First); and Beverly Ledbetter, longstanding General Counsel of Brown University, who infused in me a practical and thorough appreciation for the necessity of a firm grounding in the law to apply compliance and ethics principles to politically and socially complex organizations.

Spiritually, two great Popes, St. John Paul II and Francis, and three great priests, Fr. Joe Mallia, Fr. Bob McCabe and Fr. Leo Sabourin, have grounded me and instructed me in the one true faith in our Lord and Savior, Jesus Christ.

And to the many who may remain unnamed here, but who

know with certainty the uplifting impact that you have had upon my amazing life: Thank you.

Together, we have cheated Death.

ABOUT THE AUTHOR

Cris Mattoon

Born in New York in the late 1960s to two young and caring parents, Cris would move to Rhode Island with his father following his parents' divorce. Cris completed his final two years of high school in Houston, Texas, while living with his mother, before studying business at Texas A&M University, the University of Rhode Island, and Johnson & Wales University (Providence).

Cris embarked on a career in public accounting and banking, earning his Juris Doctor at Roger Williams University School of Law in Bristol, Rhode Island along the way. His love of orderly financial systems, governance standards, and regulatory compliance culminated in an exciting decades-long career leading corporate compliance and ethics efforts across multiple industries. Every action that Cris took has been with an unrelenting commitment to improving access to equal opportunity and to building diverse, equitable, and inclusive teams of leaders.

While in law school, Cris married his beautiful bride, Kimberly, and honeymooned in Walt Disney World. After moving back to Kimberly's home state of Michigan, they welcomed their precious daughter, Elizabeth a few years later. The family home has welcomed literally dozens of pets over the years from dogs and cats to guinea pigs and fish.

Active in their Church, school systems, and community, Cris has enjoyed teaching Sunday School and coaching Elizabeth and other youth in a variety of sports. Cris continues to enjoy playing golf with Elizabeth, and as an avid runner and health enthusiast, he enjoys participating in 5K events with Kimberly and family outings to their local gym.

The remainder of his amazing life has yet to be written, as Cris continues cheating Death and outrunning the Inevitable one day at a time.

Made in the USA
Columbia, SC
10 April 2021